DETERMINISM AND AMERICAN FOREIGN RELATIONS DURING THE FRANKLIN D. ROOSEVELT ERA

WAYNE S. COLE

UNIVERSITY
PRESS OF
AMERICA

Lanham • New York • London

3/013338

Copyright © 1995 by
University Press of America,® Inc.
4720 Boston Way
Lanham, Maryland 20706

3 Henrietta Street
London WC2E 8LU England

Library of Congress Cataloging-in-Publication Data

Cole, Wayne S.
Determinism and American foreign relations during the
Franklin D. Roosevelt era / by Wayne S. Cole.
p.   cm.
Includes index.
1. United States—Foreign relations—1933–1945.   2. History—
Philosophy.   3. Determinism (Philosophy)   4. Roosevelt, Franklin
D. (Franklin Delano), 1882–1945.   I. Title.
E806.C593   1995   327.73—dc20   94-32939 CIP

ISBN 0–8191–9739–4 (cloth : alk. paper)

 The paper used in this publication meets the minimum requirements of
American National Standard for Information Sciences—Permanence
of Paper for Printed Library Materials, ANSI Z39.48–1984.

Also by Wayne S. Cole

America First: The Battle Against Intervention, 1940-1941 (1953)

Senator Gerald P. Nye and American Foreign Relations (1962)

An Interpretive History of American Foreign Relations(1968,1974)

Charles A Lindbergh and the Battle Against American Intervention in World War II (1974)

Roosevelt and the Isolationists, 1932-45 (1983)

Norway and the United States, 1905-1955:Two Democracies in Peace and War (1989)

This One is For

Virginia, Tom, and Bonnie

CONTENTS

Preface

PREFACE

Franklin D. Roosevelt was one of America's most charismatic leaders. In his fourth term when he died on April 12, 1945, he served longer than any other president. Roosevelt presided during America's worst depression and during the most terrible war in human history. He inaugurated changes both at home and abroad that continue to affect Americans and others all over the world. Historians rank him as one of America's greatest presidents.

Analysts in his own time and scholars since have written thousands of books and articles trying to describe, explain, and evaluate the man and his times. One might have thought everything had been written about Roosevelt there was to write. Not so!

For nearly half a century since his death I have read, studied, taught, researched, reflected, written, and published on Roosevelt and his times. I approached him from a different background and different perspective than most. My intellectual explorations have made me increasingly skeptical of "Great Man" or "Devil" theories. I have, instead, became more persuaded of a determinist approach--both in viewing Franklin D. Roosevelt and in examining the whole human adventure.

The approach is given less to praising heroes and denouncing villains. It tries to avoid self-righteousness and strives for empathy with those who are different. "There but for the grace of God go I." It focuses on what individuals did, why they did it, and why things turned out as they did.

Though other cultures have incorporated aspects of determinism in their perspectives, the approach does not mesh well with traditional Western and American values. It does not inspire stirring images of heroism, self-reliance, and freedom of the will.

I do not expect to persuade others that I have discovered the truth on this matter. I do hope, however, that my intellectual explorations may encourage others to think more deeply on the approach and on the whole matter of causation in the human experience. Join me as I trace paths I have explored to reach this little known destination.

Wayne S. Cole

Silver Spring, Maryland
July 1, 1994

CHAPTER 1

YOU CAN'T GET HERE FROM THERE--BUT I DID![1]

This study traces the bumpy twisting paths that one historian inadvertently traveled from an unquestioning belief in freedom of the will to a belief in historical determinism. That determinism includes the conviction that circumstances--genetic, physiological, environmental, family, experiences, and conditions at home and abroad--circumstances control. Those total circumstances even control the decision-making processes that seem so free and independent from the individual's perspective.

It was not a path that I intended or wanted to follow. The destination I reached in my historiographical wanderings is not the Promised Land of the Great American Dream. In a sense the whole experience was "un-American." The paths opened up for me as I studied, taught, researched, and wrote on the history of American foreign relations, particularly on the Franklin D. Roosevelt years from 1932 to 1945.

As a small town boy in Iowa back in the 1920s and 1930s I learned that it was possible to change things, to make life better. It required hard work, education, careful planning, cooperation of others, and democracy--but it could be done. My maternal ancestors had accomplished that for themselves and their descendants when they emigrated from Norway to America. My father had done that when as an orphaned teenager he had fled poverty and deprivation in the hills of southern Indiana to the rich soils of Iowa where he made his living as a tradesman and small businessman. I had seen it happen in our small community when townspeople banded together to accomplish positive goals beneficial to the community and to those who lived there. And I read in my books of great persons in history who had, through heroic effort and great wisdom, made life better (or at least different) for their countries and the world. It could be done by the giants of the past--and perhaps by small town youngsters in Iowa as well. It was the American way.

President Roosevelt was demonstrating how it could be done by using New Deal measures to end the Great Depression. Our community

---

[1] This essay was published originally in *The Society for Historians of American Foreign Relations Newsletter* 23 (September, 1992): 17-37, and is reprinted here by permission.

saw little evidence of economic recovery, but many thought FDR was on the right track. Even if he were wrong, surely someone could restore prosperity by taking proper actions. Problems were meant to be solved through right thought and action. For me the study of history could help point the way. At least I proposed to find out.

That confidence took on more urgent and even deeply personal patterns with the eruption of World War II and the involvement of the United States in that war. Japanese military forces ignited war in East Asia in July 1937--during the summer between my freshman and sophomore years in high school. Nazi Germany set off the European war when Hitler's blitzkrieg smashed into Poland in September 1939--at the beginning of my senior year in high school. On December 7, 1941, when the Japanese attack on Pearl Harbor brought the United States into that war, I was in the middle of my sophomore year of college. It was not a good time to be a teenager. That terrible war could shatter one's dreams.

In that setting I turned to the study of diplomatic history in my quest for the wisdom and secret formulas from the past that might accomplish peace and security. I collected learned quotations that assured me that lessons for the present and future might be discovered through study of the past. And this corn-fed boy from Iowa determined to learn those vital lessons so he might more wisely help guide to a better future. That hope, that determination, persisted for years. Whether it required an improved version of Woodrow Wilson's internationalism and League of Nations, the pacifism and democratic socialism so appealing to some of my graduate professors, the practical realism urged by political science professors, or some formula as yet undiscovered, it could be found and, God willing, could be implemented. Progress was inevitable and sooner or later solutions would be at hand. This might be the time. I determined to play a role in making that dream a reality.

That was where things stood when I laid down my duties as a military officer and pilot in the Army Air Force in 1945 at the close of World War II. Graduation from college in 1946 and service as a high school history teacher in 1946-1947, confirmed me in that hope, that expectation, for the future.

In 1947 I began my graduate studies in American diplomatic history at the University of Wisconsin under the able direction of Professor Fred Harvey Harrington, with the accomplishment of that goal in the forefront of my thinking.[2] Also on the faculty there was the Pulitzer-prize-winning historian, Merle Curti. That gentle scholar-teacher's tone encouraged students in the quest for that better life through democratic processes. Nonetheless, there the seeds of determinism were beginning to be planted in the soil of my mind.

In his brilliant, almost casual style, Professor Harrington introduced students to interpretations of historian Charles A. Beard as those perspectives projected into foreign affairs--particularly from Beard's book, *The Idea of National Interest: An Analytical Study in American Foreign Policy*, published in 1934.[3] The book itself was poorly organized and uneven in style and analysis. But Harrington paved the way for fuller understanding of that seminal work by providing his own more clearly enunciated variations of the Beardian views in his classes.[4] The fact that that great teacher delivered his lectures without notes and with refreshing clarity made it easy for listeners to be persuaded of the validity of the ideas he advanced. In particular I remember one brilliant two-hour lecture by Harrington to his pro-seminar on "American Expansion Overseas," delivered on October 6, 1948, that put all the pieces together for me.

In brief, the Beard-Harrington analysis found the roots of American conceptions of national interest and foreign policies in the perceived self-interests of two broad socio-economic-sectional-political groupings --Alexander Hamilton's business-merchant-capitalist groups of the urban northeast, and Thomas Jefferson's farmer-agrarian groups in the rural south and west. Both groups encouraged expansion--but of two quite

---

[2] For perceptive portraits of Professor Harrington by an able historian who completed his doctorate under Harrington's direction a few years after I did, see Walter LaFeber, "Fred Harvey Harrington," *Diplomatic History* 9 (Fall, 1985): 311-19, and Walter LaFeber, "Fred Harvey Harrington, Teacher and Friend: An Appreciation," in Thomas J. McCormick and Walter LaFeber, ed., *Behind the Throne: Servants of Power to Imperial Presidents, 1898-1968* (Madison: University of Wisconsin Press, 1993), 3-19.

[3] Charles A. Beard with the collaboration of G. H. E. Smith, *The Idea of National Interest: An Analytical Study in American Foreign Policy* (New York: Macmillan Co., 1934).

[4] For a brief article by Harrington on Beard's book, see Fred Harvey Harrington, "Beard's Idea of National Interest and New Interpretations," *American Perspectives: A Quarterly Analysis of Foreign Policy* 4 (Fall, 1950): 335-45.

different sorts.[5] The urban business groups looked abroad to commercial-creditor expansion overseas. That Hamiltonian urban business and capitalist expansion laid the groundwork for what became in the twentieth century America's overseas empire and worldwide internationalism. In contrast, the farmer-agrarian groups looked westward for lands and continental security. Thomas Jefferson served that continental expansionism through the Louisiana Purchase of 1803. That continental orientation included a distrust of Europe in general and of England in particular that came to be known in the twentieth century as American "isolationism"--nonintervention in Europe and rejection of foreign entanglements.

The particular foreign policies of the United States at any given time depended upon which of the two broad socio-economic groups, in their continuing struggles against each other, happened to be dominant or in power at that time. When he wrote his book in 1934 Beard thought he saw a merging of those two groups of interests in early phases of the Roosevelt New Deal.[6] When it became apparent later, however, that FDR's foreign policies were more consistent with Hamilton's way than with Jefferson's, Beard parted company with Roosevelt (and with the dominant forces in American society and economy by that time). As a result Beard unintentionally self-destructed. His standing as a historian had largely been destroyed by the time he died in 1948.

That Beard-Harrington analysis underscored domestic socio-economic bases for American foreign policy, but it also included emphasis on geographic bases for differences on foreign affairs. That opened the door for the contributions of historian Frederick Jackson Turner who had taught many years at Wisconsin and later at Harvard. Turner's emphasis on sectional and frontier influences had not focused particularly on foreign affairs. Nonetheless, his approach had foreign policy implications that he and others recognized.[7] Harrington had read Turner, but Turner's impact on my thinking was pressed more

---

[5] Beard, *Idea of National Interest*, passim, but see particularly 47-54, 84-88, 549-53.

[6] Ibid., 552-53.

[7] Frederick Jackson Turner, *The Frontier in American History* (New York: Henry Holt & Co., 1920); and Frederick Jackson Turner, *The Significance of Sections in American History* (New York: Henry Holt & Co., 1932).

explicitly by other professors at Wisconsin--Merle Curti,[8] William B. Hesseltine,[9] and Merrill Jensen.[10] That Turner emphasis fit nicely with the Beard-Harrington analysis of the history of foreign relations.

In my undergraduate studies I had mastered the main details of the history of American foreign relations. But those details left me asking, "So what? What does it all mean?" The Beard-Turner analyses, as channeled through Harrington, Curti, Hesseltine, and Jensen, answered those questions for me powerfully and persuasively. Through all of that there was the implication that that American expansion (of whichever variety) was less than wise in terms of peace and security. And there was, I thought, the implication (made explicit in Beard's companion book, *The Open Door at Home*) that some form of democratic socialism with its emphasis on domestic socio-economic planning and with minimal reliance on overseas activity and expansion provided the greatest hope for peace and security for the United States--and possibly, by example, for the rest of the world.[11] I had my historically based "secret formula" for peace and security.

In 1950 I went off to my first full-time university teaching position at the University of Arkansas. The courses I taught there in the midst of the Ozark mountains of northwest Arkansas were straight Beard-Harrington-Curti et al. It all fit together perfectly. I had already made the first steps toward determinism--without realizing what I had done. I did so without questioning in the slightest my continued faith in the ability of informed persons, with clear historical awareness, to guide America and the world toward enlightened peace and security.

---

[8] Merle Curti, "The Section and the Frontier in American History: The Methodological Concepts of Frederick Jackson Turner," in *Methods in Social Science: A Case Book*, ed. Stuart Rice (Chicago: University of Chicago Press, 1931), 353-67; and Merle Curti, "Frederick Jackson Turner, 1861-1932," in Merle Curti, *Probing Our Past* (New York: Harper & Brothers, 1955), 32-55.

[9] William B. Hesseltine, "Regions, Classes and Sections in American History," *Journal of Land and Public Utilities* 20 (February, 1944): 35-44.

[10] Merrill Jensen, ed., *Regionalism in America* (Madison and Milwaukee: University of Wisconsin Press, 1965), xv-xvi, 3-4.

[11] Charles A. Beard with the collaboration of G. H. E. Smith, *The Open Door at Home: A Trial Philosophy of National Interest* (New York: Macmillan Co., 1934). See also Beard, *Idea of National Interest*, 552.

Other variables gradually were added to that intellectual compound that strengthened the still unrecognized determinist element in my evolving thinking. For example, Albert K. Weinberg's book, *Manifest Destiny: A Study of Nationalist Expansionism in American History*, cranked the spirit of nationalism and ideas into the mix. As Merle Curti had done in his studies of intellectual history, Weinberg demonstrated the intimate relationship between interests and ideas. He did so without cynically suggesting that the ideas were hypocritical or that ideas were not real forces in their own right. As Weinberg phrased it, "Moral ideology was the partner of self-interest in the intimate alliance of which expansionism was the offspring." Throughout Weinberg was "conceding sincerity to ideology but assuming its unconscious determination by self-interest."[12]

Thomas A. Bailey of Stanford University was the author of the textbook used in the first course I took as an undergraduate on diplomatic history, *A Diplomatic History of the American People*. First published in 1940, it went through ten editions before its author died in 1983.[13] As student or teacher I used the first seven and the last editions of that popular textbook. Bailey emphasized the impact of public opinion (often ill-informed or misinformed) on foreign affairs. He advanced his interpretation even more clearly and persuasively in his book, *The Man in the Street: The Impact of American Public Opinion on Foreign Policy*, published in 1948. The topical chapters in that free-wheeling book were weak on the socio-economic-geographic influences so powerful in the approaches of Beard-Harrington-Curti et al. But it successfully highlighted various other domestic variables--

---

[12]   Albert K. Weinberg, *Manifest Destiny: A Study of Nationalist Expansionism in American History* (Baltimore: Johns Hopkins Press, 1935), 12, 38.

[13]   Thomas A. Bailey, *A Diplomatic History of the American People*, 10th ed. (Englewood, N.J.: Prentice-Hall, Inc., 1980). See also, Thomas A. Bailey, *The American Pageant Revisited: Recollections of a Stanford Historian* (Stanford, California: Hoover Institution Press, 1982); Alexander DeConde and Armin Rappaport, "Biographical Introduction," in *Essays Diplomatic and Undiplomatic of Thomas A. Bailey*, eds. Alexander DeConde and Armin Rappaport (New York: Appleton-Century-Crofts, 1969), vii-xiii; and Raymond G. O'Connor, "Thomas A. Bailey: His Impact," *Diplomatic History* 9 (Fall, 1985): 303-309.

notably ethnic influences. It also included chapters on ideological, political, and even religious influences. He wrote of the roles of the press and radio in shaping thinking on foreign affairs.[14] Bailey's treatment of the impact of public opinion on foreign affairs forced me to broaden the socio-economic-sectional emphases I had brought with me from Wisconsin to Arkansas, and then took with me in the middle of the 1950s to Iowa State University in central Iowa.

In Iowa two quite different major developments moved me further down the paths toward historical determinism. One deepened an aspect of the Beard-Harrington interpretation, and the other provided a comprehensive theoretical construct for viewing and understanding the history of foreign relations.

The first grew out of my research on Gerald P. Nye, Republican senator from North Dakota. It was an expansion of my earlier research and writing on the America First Committee. In my thesis and dissertation on America First I had taken brief looks at the foreign policy views of Senator Nye in 1941. In that context he appeared like one of several conservative Republican isolationists from the middle west and great plains who had opposed President Roosevelt's foreign policies.[15]

While in Arkansas, far from essential manuscript collections, I had studied Nye's career in periodicals available there.   I quickly discovered that despite his conservative image by 1941, during the greater part of his public career Nye had been a progressive and had supported much of FDR's New Deal. In tracing the evolution of his thought and politics I noted the senator's changing attitudes toward presidential power in general and Roosevelt's power in particular. I thought I saw in those changing attitudes the "hinges" by which the North Dakota senator swung from his earlier progressivism toward conservatism--all the while retaining his isolationism.

When I got to Iowa State (still far from essential archives and manuscripts) I resolved to test my theory by tracing Nye's views

---

[14] Thomas A. Bailey, *The Man in the Street: The Impact of American Public Opinion on Foreign Policy* (New York: Macmillan Co., 1948).

[15] Wayne S. Cole, *America First: The Battle Against Intervention, 1940-1941* (Madison: University of Wisconsin Press, 1953), 23, 39, 45, 56, 58, 110, 129, 140, 156, 161, 170, 187, 188, 264. For my later perspectives on America First see chapter 4 of this book.

through the twenty years of his senate career by studying his speeches published in the *Congressional Record*. At Iowa State in the 1950s those massive volumes were stored in a poorly heated metal warehouse. To use them I had to get a special key for the building, place my trusty Smith-Corona typewriter on a high metal shelf, prop myself up by sitting on a couple of volumes of the *Record* piled on a rickety chair, and go to work. Through long hours and days those volumes allowed me to move mentally back to the United States senate of the 1920s, 1930s, and 1940s. And the outlines of my theory on the significance of changing attitudes toward presidential power (modified in the process) gradually fell into place.

As the days and weeks passed, however, a new and quite unexpected theme began to emerge from my researches. I found thoughts and patterns in Senator Nye's speeches that sounded surprisingly familiar. And I came to realize that they were the agrarian thoughts I had studied long before in the person of Virginia's Thomas Jefferson and, in different terms, in Nebraska's Populist-Democratic William Jennings Bryan.

It was not far fetched to link Nye of North Dakota with Bryan of Nebraska. Neither had won the hero's mantle in America's folklore. And after Pearl Harbor (and even before) leading isolationists (including both Beard and Nye) had been discredited in public and professional eyes. The beating that Nye and his fellow isolationists had taken at the hands of Roosevelt and the interventionists before and during World War II had left his public image badly battered.

To link the besmirched Nye with one of America's most honored Founding Fathers, Thomas Jefferson, seemed shocking to many. There was no way that that learned and beloved author of America's magnificent Declaration of Independence could be linked a century and one-half later with the rustic discredited Republican senator from the dusty great plains state of North Dakota. It could not be.

Nonetheless, when one put the two men under the research microscope the fundamental similarities were there. Both Jefferson and Nye emerged from agricultural sectors of America's society and economy. Both spoke out for an agrarian-based democracy. Both were critical of political dominance by urban business and creditor interests. Both distrusted foreign policy projections of the economic interests of those urban groups. Both were critical of big navy interests. Both distrusted Great Britain. Both saw America's national interests as predominantly continental with emphasis on North America. Both opposed "entangling alliances." Both treasured the culture and values they associated with rural America. There were differences between Jefferson and Nye, of course, but when one analyzed the socio-economic bases for the views of the two men the lines of continuity were striking. And that fitted perfectly with the Hamilton-Jefferson Beard-Harrington analysis of the socio-economic bases for the history of American foreign relations.

For that small-town young man pounding away on his portable typewriter in that old warehouse at Iowa State, the discovery was nothing short of sensational. It matters not that it may have been "old hat" to more sophisticated and learned scholars. It matters not that others may have found the discovery either mistaken or unimportant. For me (then and since) it has been one of the most exciting and revealing intellectual discoveries of my lifetime. (See chapter 3) When, through further research, I found that Nye in his agrarian Jeffersonian perspective was only one among a whole passel of western agrarian progressives whose domestic views projected into isolationist perspectives in foreign affairs, it made the findings even more exciting for me.[16]

Later I met the former senator, did research in the personal papers he had stored in his suburban Maryland home, and studied the newspapers that he had edited as a young man in Wisconsin, Iowa, and North Dakota. But I made my central discovery in that old warehouse while pouring over the senator's speeches printed in the *Congressional Record*. The book I subsequently wrote, *Senator Gerald P. Nye and American Foreign Relations*, was published in 1962. It was the most intellectually exciting accomplishment of my professional career.[17] The whole experience reinforced my convictions on the soundness of the Beard-Harrington analysis of socio-economic bases for foreign policies.

---

[16] Wayne S. Cole, *Roosevelt and the Isolationists, 1932-45* (Lincoln: University of Nebraska Press, 1983), passim, but see especially 8, 34-38, 50, 128-29.

[17] Wayne S. Cole, *Senator Gerald P. Nye and American Foreign Relations* (Minneapolis: University of Minnesota Press, 1962), passim, but see particularly chapters 1 and 13.

If that analysis of Nye and more generally on the Beard-Harrington interpretation were correct, then the rise and fall of the foreign policy projections of those agrarian socio-economic interests lay less in the talents or wisdom of those agrarian spokesmen than in the power (or lack of power) those agrarian interests commanded within the United States relative to the urban business-commercial-creditor interests. Insofar as that may have been true, then it was, broadly speaking, the ever conquering industrial revolution and the accompanying urbanization of American society that accounted for the rise of American overseas imperialism and internationalism, and for the decline of America's traditional isolationism. Circumstances were controlling rather more than the wisdom and political skills of individual Americans. Now that was getting terribly close to determinism in foreign affairs--whether that skinny young history professor in Iowa realized it or not!

At the same time that I was making those interpretive discoveries on agrarian bases for the rise and fall of isolationism, I was also shaping a more generalized paradigm to explain the history of American foreign relations. My studies through the early 1950s had accounted for the general outlines of domestic influences on the history of American foreign relations, and for the continuity of expansion in foreign affairs. But all of that gave little attention to the world scene--to England's George III, France's Napoleon, Germany's Kaiser William II and Adolf Hitler, Britain's Winston Churchill, the Soviet Union's Joseph Stalin, and China's Mao Tse-tung. They were all there, but the Beard-Harrington-Cole perspectives on American foreign affairs might not have been radically different even if they had not been. The dominant domestic influences projected into foreign affairs mattered most--not overseas challenges or threats to national security and survival.

Enter Professor Hans J. Morgenthau of the University of Chicago and his fellow "Realists." I had taken world politics courses as an undergraduate, had taught high school government, and had minored in political science-international relations in graduate school. I had read Walter Lippmann, Nicholas J. Spykman, and George F. Kennan. But it had not really "taken" in my mind; I thought they were "missing the point" that my history professors at Wisconsin had elucidated so clearly.

When I moved to Iowa State, however, I was required to teach political science courses on World Politics and International Organization and on International Relations, as well as history courses.

In those days that made it imperative that I read and understand what Professor Morgenthau and his fellow "Realists" had to tell me. Of seminal importance was Morgenthau's volume, *Politics Among Nations; The Struggle for Power and Peace.*[18] I quickly learned that if a reader accepted Morgenthau's assumptions and definitions, and if one followed his logic closely, one was likely to be hooked. Morgenthau's brilliant mind could overpower the reader.

In addition, Morgenthau's perspectives had an enthusiastic spokesman in the person of Professor Norman A. Graebner, one of my more talented colleagues at Iowa State. Graebner had studied at the University of Chicago, had became a doctrinaire "Realist," and was a devoted disciple of Morgenthau. In a sense Graebner was to my study of Morgenthau and the Realists what Harrington had been to my study of Beard. Morgenthau and Graebner could not compel me to turn away from my earlier perspectives, but they did lead me to add important new dimensions to my analysis.

Professor Morgenthau wrote about power. That was not new. I already knew that the struggle for power within the United States between the urban business groups and the rural farming groups determined which would define American policies at home and abroad. But in the hands of Morgenthau power became all. "The objectives of foreign policy must be defined in terms of national interest and must be supported with adequate power."[19] "Diplomacy without power is feeble, and power without diplomacy is destructive and blind."[20] Power was not intrinsically good or bad, wise or unwise; it simply was. Nothing good or bad, wise or unwise, could prevail without supporting power broadly defined. A state's power was always relative to the power of the states with which it was dealing. Morgenthau defined power broadly, including geography, natural resources, industrial capacity, military preparedness, population, national character, national morale, quality of government, and quality of

---

[18] Hans J. Morgenthau, *Politics Among Nations: The Struggle for Power and Peace* (New York: Alfred A. Knopf, 1954).

[19] Ibid., 528.

[20] Hans J. Morgenthau, *In Defense of National Interest: A Critical Examination of American Foreign Policy* (New York: Alfred A. Knopf, Inc., 1952), 242.

diplomacy.[21] That ever present role of power determined patterns in world affairs far more than law, morality, international organization, or world opinion. In Morgenthau's view there was no hope for actions or objectives not supported with adequate power.

Room for maneuver by world leaders lay in their techniques for maximizing and martialling power, and in diplomacy backed by power. Morgenthau's rules for diplomacy provided no hope for utopian solutions not backed with sufficient power.[22] Professor Morgenthau, more than any other scholar, sensitized me to the role of power and to external influences on foreign affairs. He and his fellow Realists provided missing pieces for my formula for understanding the history of foreign relations.

Consequently by 1957 I was ready to put all the pieces together in a complete restructuring of my courses on the history of American foreign relations. The hypothesis that I began using as the format for my diplomatic history courses at that time was expressed simply and compactly: American foreign affairs are the product of both external influences in the drive for peace and security, and of internal influences in the efforts to satisfy the needs and desires of the dominant groups within the United States. Those external and internal influences could take many forms and have many different consequences, but one of the frequently encountered consequences of those influences was expansion by the United States in one form or another.

In that construct the emphasis on external influences grew out of the intellectual input of Morgenthau and other Realists. The domestic influences (social, economic, political, ideological, and military) grew out of the intellectual input of Beard, Harrington, Curti, Weinberg, Bailey, and others. The theme of expansion was straight Harrington.

To visualize my hypothesis I used a parallelogram with one vector symbolizing external influences, the other vector symbolizing domestic influences, and the resultant of those two vectors including a prominent element of expansion. I then divided the history of American foreign relations into six chronological periods. The first lecture for each period described the world scene with emphasis on changing power relationships. The second lecture described domestic circumstances within the United States that affected policies abroad. Then followed

---

[21] Morgenthau, *Politics Among Nations*, 102-37.

[22] Ibid., 526-35.

lectures that traced the actual course of foreign affairs in that period, with emphasis on the controlling external and internal influences and on the contributions of those two categories of influences on American expansion. It was impossible for any historian to know all the variables involved, but for me the hypothesis accounted for nearly everything that went into shaping the history of foreign affairs--except people.

The first time I used that hypothesis and its parallelogram to introduce my course on the history of American foreign relations one of my brighter graduate students challenged it (and me). A doctoral student in economics, he was accustomed to the use of statistical methods. He thought the general logic of my hypothesis was reasonable and useful intellectually. But he objected to my use of the parallelogram. He contended that the parallelogram implied that there was one fixed resultant of the external and internal influences operating on foreign affairs in any particular situation. That fixed resultant left no room for the possibility of freedom of will, or for choice among alternative courses of action. In other words he objected to the determinism implied by my hypothesis and parallelogram. He suggested that rather than using the geometric figure I should shift to the statistician's figure of speech. Given certain external influences, and given certain domestic influences, there was a high statistical probability that one outcome would prevail and that others would not. But those probabilities did not rule out alternative courses--however unlikely. That statistical language left room for the possibility of freedom of choice--albeit within confines narrowed by statistical probabilities. The student and I both realized that historians and statesmen lacked the capacity for the geometric or statistical precision that either of the figures of speech implied. I was grateful for the student's contribution. At that time I had no intention of ruling out freedom of choice or the individual's control over destiny--though I realized that the rigidity of my format narrowed the range for choices considerably.

I labored long and hard to prepare lectures consistent with my hypothesis. Students found it helpful. It made sense of episodes that were less meaningful without its help. And for me it turned on lights all over the place.

If the idea was intellectually sound and helpful, perhaps others might benefit if I put it in the form of a textbook on the history of American foreign affairs. I approached publishers, found some interest, signed an agreement with Dorsey Press, and began converting my lectures into chapters for a textbook. (See chapter 2)

It was then that I left Iowa State University in 1965 and took a position at the University of Maryland, just outside of Washington, D. C. That move allowed me to teach exclusively in the field of American diplomatic history, work more with graduate students, and move closer to the rich research facilities in the Library of Congress, National Archives, and other manuscript depositories in the eastern part of the United States. I proposed to make the best possible use of the opportunities that my new position made available, within the limits of my energies and abilities. It was, for me, the culmination of my professional ambitions.

When I began my duties at the University of Maryland I continued to convert my lectures into chapters for the diplomatic history textbook for which I had contracted, while at the same time using those same lectures for the classes I was teaching. Dorsey Press published my book, *An Interpretive History of American Foreign Relations*, in 1968 and a revised edition in 1974.[23] I was pleased with it, most of my students liked it, and it won respectable numbers of adoptions.

Since my lectures were then in the textbook that I was using for my course, I had to decide how to handle my class lectures at that juncture. One of my graduate students at Maryland inadvertently gave me the idea for handling that problem. He told me that he thought my lectures (i.e. the lectures I was at that moment converting into a textbook) were "history without heroes." He probably did not know that that description had been applied long before to Charles A. Beard and others.

In any event, when students began using my textbook, I began using a biographical approach in my lectures. At each class meeting I lectured on a different individual who was significant in the history of American foreign relations. I divided each lecture into four parts: First, an introduction and overview showing how the individual had significance in broader patterns of the history of foreign relations; second, a biographical sketch of the individual's background, values, methods, and style; third, a summary of the individual's specific roles

---

[23] Wayne S. Cole, *An Interpretive History of American Foreign Relations* (Homewood, Illinois: Dorsey Press, 1968), rev. ed. (Homewood, Illinois: Dorsey Press, 1974).

in foreign affairs; and finally, a conclusion underscoring the significance of the individual in American foreign relations.

I really threw myself into the task of preparing those biographical lectures. I read more biographies than I had ever read before--and delighted in doing so. It was fun and intellectually exciting both to prepare and to present the lectures. Most students understood how the lectures and the text were supposed to compliment each other.

Courses on great people tend toward "Great Man" or "Devil" theories of history. I almost expected that to happen with the biographical lectures I prepared and presented at Maryland beginning in 1968. Nonetheless, in practice the opposite pattern evolved in my lectures--and in my intellectual development. It is impossible for the biographer to know all the subtle variables that go into making an individual. But by the time I understood an individual well and had sketched the person's background and values for a given lecture, that individual's actual conduct in foreign affairs fell naturally into the patterns one should have expected.   There were, for me, no real surprises. That was true whether I was lecturing on such giants as Hamilton, Jefferson, John Quincy Adams, Webster, Polk, Seward, Theodore Roosevelt, Wilson, or Franklin D. Roosevelt, or on more obscure persons such as Nicholas P. Trist, William Walker, Cassius M. Clay, John A. Kasson, Horace N. Allen, or John L. Stevens. I worried that in my eagerness to fit individuals into my hypothesis I may have been bending and squeezing them into unnatural forms.   But I persuaded myself that I was not doing that.

Consequently the combination of using my textbook and its hypothesis, along with my biographical lectures, had the effect of moving my thinking further and further in determinist directions. Then, for the first time, I became troubled by the determinism in my thinking. I sometimes expressed my uneasiness about the role of determinism in my historiographical thinking and invited counter arguments from students and colleagues. None could dissuade me. One semester I even gave a special course that I called "Heroes and Determinism in the History of American Foreign Relations." But it failed to disabuse me.

In the spring of 1990 I delivered a major lecture on our campus on, "Franklin D. Roosevelt: Great Man or Man for His Times," in which I advanced the most fully developed determinist interpretation I had ever presented. (See chapter 5) In that lecture I said: "Each individual (no matter how great or obscure) is a product of, is shaped by, his or her background, experiences, opportunities, environment, and times. No individual has any control over whether he or she will be born or not, or over the time, place, or circumstances of that birth--whether in primitive pre-historic times or in modern America, whether into Western Civilization or into one of the non-Western cultures. No one has the slightest control over his or her genetic inheritance: the physical, mental, and emotional equipment with which the individual is endowed genetically. One has no control over the choice of one's race, ethnic background, or sex. The child cannot choose his or her parents, family, socio-economic class level, initial religious training, or educational opportunities, facilities, or teachers. Few of us depart very radically from the patterns and directions set for us by our backgrounds, families, and environments. Even as adults one may have little or no control over one's natural energies or body chemistry that may affect personality, emotions, and general effectiveness." I concluded that "Franklin D. Roosevelt was the right person in the right place at the right time--but circumstances in his background, within the United States, and on the world scene made his times; FDR did not." The lecture went well, but most who discussed the issue with me parted company so far as determinism was concerned--without persuading me that I was mistaken.

Now here I stand at the end (or at very nearly the end) of my intellectual journey. I cannot with certainty prove that my analysis is correct. One can never know all the relevant variables that go into making an individual, or all the functional variables at home and abroad. My analysis is not emotionally satisfying and is not consistent with the near-universal assumptions prevailing among the American people (and scholars). Nonetheless, at the present state of historical methodology, I am persuaded that scholars cannot, with certainty, prove that I am wrong.

CHAPTER 2

AN APPROACH TO THE STUDY OF AMERICAN FOREIGN RELATIONS[1]

International relations as the twentieth century nears its close challenge human capacities for wisdom, creativity, and survival. Power imbalances arouse fears for national security. Economic activities provide both bonds and friction between peoples. The self-righteousness and intolerance of conflicting ideologies make accommodation difficult. Emotions attached to the symbols of state, nation, ideology, race, or religion immeasurably complicate the task of obtaining international order. Thermonuclear weapons make "power politics" a decidedly deadly "game." The explosiveness of contemporary world affairs urgently requires statesmen and citizens to demonstrate more wisdom, judgment, and self-discipline than did those of previous generations. No tool of thought or action should be neglected if it contributes, however slightly, to the understanding and responsible control of world affairs.

One such tool is history. Knowledge about the past inevitably is fragmentary and imperfect. Facilities for measuring causes, consequences, and wisdom are pitifully crude and imprecise. Consequently, readers should not expect any historical interpretation or approach to provide perfect truth or "solutions." The finest of historical interpretations can be no more than aids in the search for understanding. Nevertheless, perceptive study of history can throw meaningful light on patterns of the past, realities of the present, and the possibilities for the future.

The general interpretive approach in this essay may be stated very briefly: America's role in world affairs has been the product of both international and domestic influences--both external and internal influences. The results of those two categories of influences have varied widely, but one of the frequent and important characteristics of those results has been American expansion in one form or another. This hypothesis has three parts--external influences, internal influences, and expansion. Each of these requires elaboration.

---

[1] This chapter was published earlier in Wayne S. Cole, *An Interpretive History of American Foreign Relations*, revised ed. (Homewood, IL: Dorsey Press, 1974), 1-16.

EXTERNAL INFLUENCES

The foreign policies of the United States (and of all other states) were designed partly to cope with the actions of other countries in the international community. The United States (like other states) has had two primary objectives in dealing with external conditions. One of those has been peace. Peace, however, was rarely if ever the only goal or even the dominant one. No state would have to go to war if it were determined that avoiding war was its sole or dominant objective. Any state could avoid war by refraining from making demands and by yielding to all demands by others. Such a course, however, would not be consistent with national survival. Wars begin when people and their governments decide that there are certain things more important than peace. America has been involved in every major world war fought since the first permanent English colony was established in the Western Hemisphere in 1607. In addition, the United States has fought regional wars and engaged in military actions without the formality of a declaration of war.

The second objective of the United States (and of other states) in dealing with external conditions is variously called national security, self-preservation, or survival. The government of every state has an obligation to protect its security and insure survival of the state. National security has always been a fundamental objective of the United States. The pursuit of that goal may have a peaceful and "live-and-let-live" quality about it. But the drive for security can easily be converted into something that is aggressive, expansionist, and warlike. It can be used to justify expansion to get more defensible boundaries or to prevent another state from seizing strategic positions. Conceivably the drive for national security could even be used to justify a "preventive war." And if national security is defined very broadly--including preservation of domestic institutions, economic prosperity, ideological and religious beliefs, and the power of particular leaders and groups-- then the drive for security conceivably could be used to justify almost any kind of action in world affairs.

Power plays a more conspicuous role in the relations between states in the international community than it normally plays in the relations between individual humans. Idealists often urge the abandonment of "power politics." The fact remains, however, that power has played a conspicuous role in international affairs, it does play such a role, and in one way or another it will continue to play a role in the future. It is not possible to eliminate power from human affairs. The need is to so organize and use power as to render maximum benefits for the people of the world. The absence of an effective world government capable of enforcing order among states partly accounts for the prominent role of national power in international affairs. Despite the United Nations, there is no policeman on the corner to regulate relations between states and to protect the weak against the strong. In the relative international anarchy that prevails, ultimately a sovereign state's survival, its success or failure, is dependent upon its power relative to that of the states with which it is dealing. One might wish it were not so, but it is, and will continue to be so long as the multistate system prevails and so long as there is no world government.

Military forces are essential for national power. But a state's power involves much more than simply the size and effectiveness of its armed forces. The power of a state in international affairs includes everything that helps it to achieve its goals minus everything that inhibits its efforts to obtain its objectives. The elements of national power include geography, natural resources, industrial capacity, military preparedness, population, national character, national morale, quality of government, and quality of diplomacy. National power is always relative to that of the states with which it is dealing. A state's power may vary on different issues and in different parts of the world. Today the United States is the world's strongest state, but during the first century of its independent history America was not powerful relative to the major states of Europe. In a direct confrontation the United States could not match such giants as Britain or France. Fortunately for the United States, however, the great powers in the eighteenth and nineteenth centuries were often preoccupied with their problems in Europe and elsewhere. Consequently, the power they brought to bear in their dealings with the United States was distinctly limited, particularly in the Western Hemisphere. "Europe's distresses spelled America's successes" often in the early diplomatic history of the United States. In any event, America's role in world affairs becomes meaningful partly in terms of its efforts to protect peace and security in the face of actions by other states in the international community.

INTERNAL INFLUENCES

In addition, American foreign policies (and those of other states as well) were partly the result of internal influences. Undoubtedly statesmen, diplomats, and military leaders often wish those domestic influences did not operate. They sometimes contend that domestic matters should not intrude into foreign affairs. But such views are essentially unrealistic. Internal conditions have affected American foreign affairs in the past, they do now, and they will in the future. It is not possible (even in a dictatorship) to eliminate domestic considerations completely. The most one might do is to guide such influences in directions that are not inconsistent with national welfare. Domestic affairs and foreign affairs are intimately related to each other. Numerically the overwhelming majority of the contacts between people in different countries are the extension of the day to day economic, social, and cultural activities of those people. Many of the policies of every state in international affairs grow partly out of the needs, desires, and ambitions of the dominant individuals and groups within that country. The specific objectives and actions of the United States in foreign affairs might be quite different if another group with different values, interests, or ambitions were in power at a particular time.

Countless domestic considerations may affect foreign policy views. Politics may be involved--the hope that a particular foreign policy may win votes or weaken political opponents. Economic interests may be important. One cannot explain all human attitudes and actions exclusively in economic terms. But individuals and groups may be more attracted by foreign policies that might benefit them financially than by policies restricting their opportunities for economic gain. Groups have not been reluctant to seek government help for their economic activity in foreign affairs. Various economic groups may have quite different views on foreign affairs, partly because of their diverse interests. Ethnic ties may be important. Sympathies of immigrants or descendants of immigrants (i.e. "hyphenated Americans") for their original mother country or their hostility for enemies of their mother country may greatly affect their attitudes on particular issues. Even religious beliefs and affiliations may cause Americans of one particular faith or another to take stands on foreign policies that may differ from the attitudes of people of different faiths. Missionary activities may directly affect their views. Ideas represent another powerful domestic influence. One cannot explain all foreign policies in ideological terms, but neither can one get an accurate understanding if ideological considerations are omitted. And finally, the emotions and psychological makeup of individual Americans and groups of Americans represent a particularly significant category of domestic influences. Leaders with different psychological and reaction patterns might follow quite different policies in the same situations. Once emotions are aroused, they can be extremely powerful influences on foreign affairs. In any event, foreign affairs and domestic affairs are intimately related, and America's role in world affairs becomes meaningful partly in terms of these internal influences.

In at least two ways power plays a fundamental role in domestic influences, just as it is basic to external considerations. First, power in its broadest sense determines which individuals and groups become dominant within a state, which are able to make their views prevail in shaping domestic and foreign policies. The internal struggle for power often is conducted politely and legally. The methods may be quite moral and ethical. Normally it is accomplished without physical violence. But the struggle goes on just the same, and its outcome determines whose interests and wishes will best be served in both domestic and foreign affairs. Second, just as a state's security in international relations cannot be assured without power, so the desires of domestic groups cannot prevail abroad without effective supporting power.

AMERICAN EXPANSION

Unfortunately, historians do not have facilities for measuring historical forces with the accuracy of a physicist. But if they had that capacity, they might explain much of American foreign relations in terms of external and internal influences. The approach may be visualized in geometric terms. That is, if the external and internal influences are the forces acting on foreign affairs (i.e. the vectors in a parallelogram), then America's policies and actions in foreign affairs represent the resultant of those two categories of influences. Historians cannot measure either the force or direction of those influences (vectors) or actions (resultants) with such precision. But if they could they might throw much additional light on America's role in world affairs.

In at least one extremely important aspect, however, that geometric figure is not satisfactory. The use of the parallelogram implies a determined or fixed resultant. Such may be the case. But those forces operate through living human beings who presumably have a capacity for choice among alternative courses of action. Particular conditions (domestic and foreign) may greatly affect their choices, but those conditions may not absolutely determine one particular choice. Consequently, in some respects the language of the statistician may be more appropriate than that of the geometrician. The statistical term "probability" seems relevant. Given certain influences (external and internal) operating on an individual or group of individuals, there may be a high degree of probability that one alternative may be selected in preference to others and quite improbable that other alternatives will be chosen. Emphasis on impersonal forces should not obscure the role of the individual personality. At the same time, however, recognition of the importance of "freedom of the will" should not hide the fact that conditions (external and internal) increase tremendously the probability that certain alternatives may be chosen in preference to others.

The exact nature of the internal and external influences has changed constantly. Consequently, the direction and force of the resultant (i.e. the policies and actions) varied widely. Nevertheless, among others one particular characteristic of that resultant stood out prominently and frequently. One of the most constant themes in the history of American foreign affairs was expansion in one form or another. From the time of the first permanent English colony in 1607 until the present moment American history has been characterized by almost continuous expansion. Expansion included every activity by which the United States increased its influence or control in other parts of the world. Sometimes that was territorial and colonial expansion--including the movement across the North American continent and the acquisition of colonies and protectorates overseas. But often American expansion was nonterritorial. Sometimes it was expansion of trade and investments. Sometimes it was expansion through religious organizations and missionary activities. There was intellectual, cultural, and ideological expansion. The tremendous diplomatic power of the United States in the world today and the presence of American military forces in many parts of the earth are evidences of that expansion. There were times when the United States did not expand rapidly. Nevertheless, one of the most consistent and important patterns in the history of American foreign affairs was the steady growth of American power, influence, and control in other parts of the world in one way or another. And that expansion was the result of both external influences in the drive for peace and security, and internal influences in the efforts to satisfy the needs and desires of the dominant individuals and groups within the United States.

CHAPTER 3

GERALD P. NYE AND AGRARIAN BASES FOR THE RISE AND FALL OF AMERICAN ISOLATIONISM[1]

On Sunday afternoon, December 7, 1941, in Pittsburgh, Pennsylvania, Republican Senator Gerald P. Nye of North Dakota addressed a large audience that had crowded into Soldiers and Sailors Memorial Hall for a meeting sponsored by the America First Committee. The lean, brown-haired midwesterner looked younger than his forty-nine years. Nye stood five feet ten and one-half inches tall and weighed less than 160 pounds. He was an unusually talented speaker. His low, resonant, almost musical voice projected an earnest intensity and conviction that moved and captivated his audience. Nye's message was of vital concern to his listeners, for he was discussing influences that he said were moving the United States ever closer to involvement in the bloody wars then raging in Europe, Africa, and Asia. He was admonishing his listeners against intervention in World War II. In the midst of his speech a reporter handed the senator a brief note informing him that Japanese military planes had attacked United States naval and air forces at Pearl Harbor in Hawaii. That shocking news brought Nye's speech and the meeting to an abrupt end.[2]

---

[1] This chapter was published earlier in John N. Schacht, ed., *Three Faces of Midwestern Isolationism: Gerald P. Nye, Robert E. Wood, John L. Lewis* (Iowa City: The Center for the Study of the Recent History of the United States, 1981), 1-20, and is reprinted here by permission.

2 Interview with Senator Gerald P. Nye, Washington, D. C., July 20, 1959; M. E. Armbruster to Page Hufty, December 11, 1941, and attached undated clipping from *Pittsburgh Press*, America First Committee Papers, Hoover Library on War, Revolution, and Peace, Stanford, California; U.S. Congress, Senate, 77th Congress, 2nd session, October 23, 1942, *Congressional Record*, 8574; and, in the Gerald P. Nye Papers, the following items: clippings from *Pittsburgh Press*, December 8, 1941, and *Pittsburgh Sun Telegraph*, December 8, 1941; John B. Gordon to Nye, December 9, 1941; Nye to Gordon, January 7, 1942; undated account of Pittsburgh America First meeting in Nye's handwriting, apparently written December 9, 1941; and memorandum, Nye to Whomsoever May be Concerned, July 3, 1969. When I researched the Nye papers they were in the Nye home in Chevy Chase, Maryland. Since that time most of those materials have been deposited in the Herbert Hoover Presidential Library, West Branch, Iowa.

It was the last of some 160 America First meetings that Senator Nye addressed. And it was the last public meeting sponsored by the isolationist America First Committee. The Japanese attack ended the Committee's long, losing battle against intervention in World War II. It very nearly ended Nye's much longer isolationist efforts. In 1944, the next time he faced election in North Dakota, voters brought his nearly twenty-year career in the United States Senate to an end.

Senator Nye was one of America's leading and most controversial isolationists, opposing intervention in foreign wars and arguing against entanglement in alliances or the League of Nations. In 1934-1936 he led the Senate Committee Investigating the Munitions Industry that was both an expression of and a force for isolationism. He was a key figure in the enactment of neutrality laws in the 1930s, helping in hundreds of speeches throughout the country to publicize and popularize noninterventionist views. He provided colorful leadership for opponents of the increasingly internationalist and interventionist policies of President Franklin D. Roosevelt. And Nye was a tireless spokesman in 1941 for the America First Committee, the leading mass pressure group battling against intervention in World War II.[3]

Senator Nye was important in his own right. But if he had been unique or "one of a kind," he would have been less significant in the history of American foreign affairs than he actually was. Insofar as Nye represented foreign policy projections of agrarian interests and values, however, he was part of long-term patterns extending back through Nebraska's William Jennings Bryan at the turn of the century to Virginia's Thomas Jefferson at the beginning of the history of the United States. Jefferson wrote that "those who labor in the earth are the chosen people of God, if ever He had a chosen people." He worried about the day in the remote future when land in America would be so filled that people would be "piled upon one another in large cities, as in Europe." Jefferson doubted that democracy could long survive in such a setting.[4] In his "Cross of Gold" oration Bryan exclaimed that

---

3 For a detailed account of Nye's life and career, see my *Senator Gerald P. Nye and American Foreign Relations* (Minneapolis: University of Minnesota Press, 1962). Much of this chapter is drawn from that book in revised form.

4 The most detailed scholarly biography of Jefferson is Dumas Malone, *Jefferson and His Times*, 5 vols. (Boston: Little, Brown, 1948-1974). See also Charles A. Beard, *Economic Origins of Jeffersonian Democracy* (New York:

"the great cities rest upon our broad and fertile prairies. Burn down your cities and leave our farms, and your cities will spring up again as if by magic; but destroy our farms and the grass will grow in the streets of every city in the country."[5] On that subject of farmers and farming, Nye spoke the language of Jefferson and Bryan with vigor and conviction. And in his own day Nye's agrarian perspectives were shared in varied degree by most of the leading Senate isolationists, including William E. Borah of Idaho, Hiram Johnson of California, George W. Norris of Nebraska, Burton K. Wheeler of Montana, Arthur Capper of Kansas, Lynn J. Frazier of North Dakota, Henrik Shipstead of Minnesota, and Robert M. La Follette, Jr. of Wisconsin.[6] Even important midwestern business men, such as General Robert E.

Macmillan, 1915), 415-67, passim; idem, *The Idea of National Interest: An Analytical Study in American Foreign Policy* (New York: Macmillan, 1934), 50-56, 84-88, 166-68, 549-51; and Gilbert Chinard, *Thomas Jefferson: The Apostle of Americanism* (2nd ed.rev.; Ann Arbor, 1957), 132-36, 211-14, 326-30,351-52, 396-99, 468-88, 491-97, passim.

5 The most detailed scholarly biography of Bryan is Paolo E. Coletta, *William Jennings Bryan*, 3 vols. (Lincoln: University of Nebraska Press, 1964-69). See also Merle Curti, *Bryan and World Peace* (Northampton: Smith College Studies in History, 1931); Paul W. Glad, *The Trumpet Soundeth: William Jennings Bryan and His Democracy,1896-1912* (Lincoln: University of Nebraska Press, 1960); and LeRoy Ashby, *William Jennings Bryan: Champion of Democracy* (Boston: Twayne Publishers, 1987).

6 I have researched the following manuscript collections on this subject: William E. Borah Papers, George W. Norris Papers, and La Follette Family Papers, all in the Library of Congress; Hiram Johnson Papers, Bancroft Library, University of California, Berkeley; Arthur Capper Papers, Kansas State Historical Society, Topeka; and Henrik Shipstead Papers, Minnesota Historical Society, St. Paul. Among the published volumes on those senators are: Robert James Maddox, *William E. Borah and American Foreign Policy* (Baton Rouge: Louisiana State University Press, 1969); Richard Lowitt, *George W. Norris*, 3 vols. (Syracuse, N.Y.: Syracuse University Press, 1963; Urbana: University of Illinois Press, 1971, 1978); Burton K. Wheeler with Paul F. Healy, *Yankee From the West: The Candid, Turbulent Life Story of the Yankee-born U.S. Senator from Montana* (Garden City, N.Y.: Doubleday & Co., 1962); Homer E. Sokolofsky, *Arthur Capper: Publisher, Politician, and Philanthropist* (Lawrence: University Press of Kansas, 1962); and Patrick J. Maney, *"Young Bob" La Follette: A Biography of Robert M. La Follette, Jr., 1895-1953* (Columbus: University of Missouri Press, 1978).

Wood of Sears, Roebuck and Company in Chicago and Henry Ford of the Ford Motor Company in Dearborn, Michigan, shared some of the perspectives that moved Nye to isolationism.[7]

Specifics varied from individual to individual, but there were common strands running through the lives and values of those and other leading isolationists. One may highlight some of those patterns by examining Nye's background, values, and activities. Born on December 19, 1892, in the small town of Hortonville, young Nye was reared in the agricultural state of Wisconsin during the Populist-Progressive era. He was guided to manhood by the example of his newspaperman father. Nye and his father followed Wisconsin's "Fighting Bob" La Follette in progressive paths. From 1911 to 1925, as an aggressive young newspaper editor, first in Wisconsin, later in Iowa, and finally in North Dakota, Gerald P. Nye crusaded for progressive reforms. As editor of the *Creston Daily Plain Dealer* in Iowa in 1915-1916, he endorsed much of President Woodrow Wilson's New Freedom program.[8]

Though Nye supported Wilson on most issues, acute agricultural difficulties in North Dakota and protests by the Nonpartisan League moved the young newspaper editor to agrarian radical political activism after World War I. Appointed to the United State Senate as a progressive Republican from North Dakota in 1925, he served nearly twenty years, until defeated near the close of World War II. In the Senate he was an insurgent Republican, agrarian progressive, a "son of the wild jackass," and an isolationist. On both domestic and foreign policy issues he worked with other western agrarian progressives, including Borah, Johnson, Norris, Capper, Wheeler, Frazier, Shipstead, and La Follette.[9]

---

7 I interviewed General Robert E. Wood in his offices in Chicago on December 23, 1947, and August 11, 1949. In 1949 General Wood allowed me to research papers relating to his role in the America First Committee that were then in his personal custody in Chicago. More recently I have researched the Wood Papers in the Herbert Hoover Presidential Library. For Ford's agrarian and rural orientation see Reynold M. Wik, *Henry Ford and Grass-roots America* (Ann Arbor: University of Michigan Press, 1972), 10-11, 105-06, 115-16, 187, 231.

8 Cole, *Gerald P. Nye*, 17-23.

9 Ibid., 24-59.

Many variables go into the making of any individual's character, style, and values. So it was with Nye. To a striking degree, however, Senator Gerald P. Nye's foreign policy views grew directly out of his agrarian radicalism and his opposition to dominance by urban industry and finance. Traditionally, the western farmer put a premium on self-reliance and hard work. But from the farmer's frame of reference, nature on the one hand and "special interests" on the other robbed him of the fruits of his labor. In coping with drought, grasshoppers, and winter storms, the farmer supplemented his labors by turning to his God and to Lady Luck. But in contending with "special interests" he increasingly turned to political action. Financiers who held the mortgage on his farm, industrialists who manufactured his equipment, railroads that carried supplies to the farmer and his products to the market, and merchants who distributed his produce all seemed, in the farmer's view, to take an unconscionably large part of the returns from his labor. And the farmer identified those "special interests" with cities --whether those cities were as nearby as Fargo, St. Paul, and Chicago, or as remote as New York and London. The farmer saw those eastern urban business interests as selfish, exploitive, and evil. They reaped where they had not sown; they enriched themselves at the expense of the farmer. And the farmer often saw the government as serving those "selfish interests" by showering special privileges upon them.

Western farmers and their political spokesmen generally did not want government ownership of the means of production and distribution. Most at that time did not even want subsidies for agriculture. But they wanted to end the special privileges of their urban exploiters. They wanted the government to restrain abuses by urban industry, railroads, and creditors so that the farmer would be charged fair prices for their services. As young Nye phrased it early in his North Dakota political career, the government should "give equal privileges to all; or take them away from those specially privileged now." Those were the circumstances and attitudes that spawned the Populist movement in the 1890s, the Nonpartisan League during and after World War I, and agrarian progressivism. In the depression decade of the 1930s they supplemented other interests in sustaining President Roosevelt's New Deal.[10]

But those agrarian considerations did not stop at the three-mile limit. When projected into foreign affairs, those same attitudes became variations of American isolationism. Most farmers (and most isolationists) were patriotic and favored building and maintaining military forces to defend American security and interests. Most farmers realized that they were affected by foreign markets and foreign suppliers. But many objected to foreign policies they believed were inspired by the same "selfish" urban interests that exploited them on the domestic scene. They objected to being taxed to pay for expensive battleships whose purpose was not so much to defend America as to subsidize eastern steel manufacturers and shipbuilders. They opposed sending those high priced ships to distant lands to defend the investments and businesses of eastern financiers. They opposed involvement in foreign wars that, in their judgment, were not essential for national security but were, instead, designed to further enrich eastern urban financiers, munitions makers, and shippers. And they resisted war propaganda that used patriotic appeals to arouse support for ventures abroad that seemed more essential to urban business interests than to American national security and freedom.

Gerald P. Nye of North Dakota fully shared those general attitudes on both domestic and foreign affairs during his years as a progressive Republican in the United States Senate. Those attitudes moved him to battle against pro-business policies of the Republican Coolidge and Hoover administrations. They led him to support much of Roosevelt's

---

10 On the Populist movement see John D. Hicks, *The Populist Revolt* (Minneapolis: University of Minnesota Press, 1931), and Lawrence Goodwyn, *The Populist Movement: A Short History of the Agrarian Revolt in America* (Oxford: Oxford University Press, 1978). On the Nonpartisan League see Robert L. Morlan, *Political Prairie Fire: The Nonpartisan League, 1915-1922* (Minneapolis: University of Minnesota Press, 1955). Broader accounts of agrarian values and activities include Russel B. Nye, *Midwestern Progressive Politics: A Historical Study of Its Origins and Development, 1870-1958* (East Lansing: Michigan State University Press, 1959), and Henry Nash Smith, *Virgin Land* (Cambridge, Mass.: Harvard University Press, 1950). The Nye quotation is from his platform, printed on letterhead stationary of the La Follette-Nye Club of Griggs County, Cooperstown, N.D., 1924, Nye Papers.

New Deal while at the same time criticizing pro-business policies of the National Recovery Administration. And those attitudes projected him into the national limelight as chairman of the Senate Special Committee Investigating the Munitions Industry in 1934-1936. Senator Nye's attacks on Wall Street's House of Morgan, on the Du Ponts and other munitions makers, and on shipbuilders were consistent with his agrarian radicalism and with that of his rural and small town constituents. Furthermore, it was logical that the neutrality legislation he proposed in the 1930s would have imposed no direct restraints on farmers but would have restricted the economic activities of urban financiers, manufacturers, and shippers. The isolationist movement was by no means exclusively rural and small town. But Gerald P. Nye and most leading Senate isolationists reflected in varied forms those agrarian values in both domestic and foreign affairs.[11]

In the 1920s and 1930s Nye and other western progressive isolationists attacked the war-making proclivities of big business and big finance. Like Thomas Jefferson long before, however, they feared bigness of almost any sort, including big military, big government, and big labor. In January, 1935, Nye said that nothing in his munitions investigation had astonished him so much as discovering that "instead of munitions-makers promoting the military activities of government, governments--especially our own war and navy departments--have been actively promoting the munitions-makers, for years." He complained of "a partnership" that the United States government had "in the business of selling American munitions of war." At that time he did not directly criticize the presidency; he sympathized with the chief executive's difficulties in withstanding pressures from powerful urban economic interests. He favored legislation limiting the president's role

---

11 I first became aware of the agrarian bases for Nye's foreign policy views and of the parallels between his perspectives and those of Jefferson and Bryan when, in 1957-58, I was researching Nye's speeches and statements in the *Congressional Record*. My intellectual groundwork for that awareness, however, had been laid earlier for me by the lectures and seminars of Professor Fred Harvey Harrington at the University of Wisconsin in 1947-50, by my study of Beard's *Idea of National Interest*, and by my observations and experiences as a boy and teenager in Iowa in the 1920s and 1930s. For details on Nye see Cole, *Gerald P. Nye*, 60-67.

in foreign affairs to help him resist such pressures.[12] By the latter part of the 1930s and on into the 1940s, however, Nye increasingly attacked the war-making proclivities of the presidency in general and of President Franklin D. Roosevelt in particular. By 1941 he denounced President Roosevelt for leading the country toward war while professing to be working for peace. He charged that the president was using dictatorial methods on the pretext of fighting dictatorships, that in fighting for the Four Freedoms abroad Americans were losing their freedoms at home. He objected to excessive presidential power in foreign affairs, to secrecy and deception. He feared that Roosevelt was deliberately using American aid to Britain short-of-war as steps-to-war, and that the president sought and hoped for shooting incidents in the Atlantic that might propel the United States into wars raging abroad.[13] Despite the attention now focused on Iowa and New Hampshire briefly during presidential primaries once every four years, in the twentieth century political parties, presidential nominations and elections, and administration policies are shaped and controlled largely by urban considerations--not by farmers or by rural and small town America.

It is easy to illustrate how Senator Nye's foreign policy attitudes fell within the framework of agrarian interests. Nye blamed American participation in World War I for many of the farmers' economic difficulties in the 1920s and 1930s, and he saw no reason to believe that American involvement in a second world war would have any better effects on the farmers's lot. The munitions investigation was a logical extension in the realm of foreign affairs of Nye's long crusade against big business, international bankers, and Wall Street. Initially the munitions investigation was at least as anti-business as it was anti-war. Later the investigation broadened its attack so that the executive branch of the government as well as big business came under fire. The neutrality laws supported by Nye imposed no significant limitations on agriculture; the self-denying provisions in the legislation applied primarily to the urban segments of the economy. For example, the arms embargo that Nye supported prohibited the export of certain types of industrial products but placed no comparable restraints on the export of agricultural and mineral products. The bans on loans and the cash-and-carry provisions inhibited urban financiers and shippers, but the

---

12 Cole, *Gerald P. Nye*, 79-96.
13 Ibid., 153-201.

effects on the farmer were indirect at most. Nye opposed large naval appropriations and thus would have restricted government "pump priming" in urban shipbuilding and steel manufacturing centers of the East. Since North Dakota got very few war contracts, limiting military appropriations might have been to its economic advantage; in effect such limitations would have reduced federal subsidies to eastern urban areas and made tax increases for North Dakota less necessary.[14]

Some of Senator Nye's proposals were never enacted; some were passed in modified form; some became law much as he wanted; and nearly all were repealed before the United States declared war in December, 1941. Recommendations by Nye that never became law included nationalizing munitions industries, taxing the profits out of war, banning the sale of non-munitions to belligerents, and a constitutional amendment that would have required a national referendum to declare war except in case of attack or immediately threatened attack by a non-American state against the Western Hemisphere. The failure to adopt much of Nye's program, and the repeal of most of the neutrality legislation before Pearl Harbor, prevented isolationists from demonstrating whether they could or could not have kept the United States out of war without endangering American security. For all practical purposes the neutrality laws were gone before Pearl Harbor.[15]

Explanations for the decline and fall of Senator Gerald P. Nye and American isolationism may be found in both international and domestic developments. On the world scene, part of the explanation may be traced to changing power relationships that undermined the comfortable security the United States had enjoyed earlier. The gradual erosion of the relative power of Great Britain and France, plus the emergence of the increasingly powerful and ambitious Germany in Europe and Japan in Asia, upset nineteenth-century security arrangements. World Wars I and II not only dramatized the deteriorating power positions of Britain and France, but contributed to their decline (and to the lessening of American national security). After World War II the weakened condition of Britain and France, the temporary eclipse of German and

---

14 Ibid., 97-132.

15 Ibid., 91-123, 153-96. The best and fullest scholarly history of the neutrality laws is Robert A. Divine, *The Illusion of Neutrality* (Chicago: University of Chicago Press, 1962).

Japanese power, and the emergence of the Soviet Union as a major world power presented the American people with an extremely disturbing international situation in which the security taken for granted in the nineteenth century was gone.

That alarming state of affairs was made more terrifying by the destructive capabilities of weapons created by science and industry and commanded by the leading adversaries in the Cold War. The first atomic bomb was not set off until after Gerald P. Nye had been retired from public life in 1945. Intercontinental bombers (even with conventional bombs) were not a practical reality during his years in the United States Senate. Nonetheless, the changes in power relationships on the world scene and the destructive capabilities of weapons developed rapidly during his public career. The disintegration of the old balance of power, the rise of aggressive challenges from the Central Powers, the Axis, and later from the Soviet Union, the creation of fantastically destructive weapons--all those developments on the world scene combined to endanger American national security and to help defeat Senator Nye and American isolationism.

The developments and conditions that doomed isolationism were not, however, limited to other parts of the world. In addition to external influences, forces within the United States also contributed to the decline of isolationism. Among those were fundamental socio-economic changes within the United States. Those changes related to the rapid urbanization of American society that accompanied the phenomenal growth of American business, industry, finance, and labor. The foreign policy views represented by Thomas Jefferson, William Jennings Bryan, and Gerald P. Nye fell into disfavor partly as a result of the rise of the city and the decline and "urbanization" of agriculture in the United States.

At the time of the first census in 1790 (when Jefferson became secretary of state), 95 percent of Americans were classified as rural, and most of them were farmers. Only about 5 percent were urban, and those Americans lived in relatively small communities by European or twentieth-century standards. Throughout American history, however, the urban population has increased at a faster rate than the rural population. Even before Nye was appointed to the Senate in 1925, the total urban population exceeded rural--though not in North Dakota. By 1994 more than three-fourths of Americans were classified as urban. Urban population and income exceeded rural in most states, including such traditionally farm states as Iowa and Nebraska. Some 20 percent of the American people lived in the "supermetropolis" extending almost continuously for some five hundred miles along the northeastern seaboard. That huge concentration of people, talent, industry, and capital exerted an influence on American thought, taste, education, national politics, and foreign policy that far exceeds its proportion of the population. Urbanization was both a cause and an effect of fundamental economic developments. When Nye became a senator the United States was already the leading industrial and financial center in the world. In 1994 less than 2 percent of the American people were farmers, and many of those got part of their incomes from non-farm sources.[16]

Farmers and farms not only declined in numbers, they also changed greatly. Science and technology revolutionized farming methods just as they affected urban manufacturing. Commercial farms grew strikingly in size, capitalization, mechanization, and production. The enlarged operations, coupled with marketing difficulties, inspired sophisticated managerial and organizational innovations that often gave the producer, processor, and distributor a community of interests cutting across rural-urban lines. The spectacular increase in grain exports in recent years gives midwestern farmers a keen awareness of the importance of foreign markets that is comparable to the awareness held by tobacco growers in the eighteenth century, by cotton planters in the nineteenth century, and by many industrialists in the twentieth century. Furthermore, the modes of living for twentieth-century commercial farmers differed little from those of persons on comparable social and economic levels in the cities. The "urbanization" of American agriculture did not wholly eliminate differences between rural and urban interests and views on foreign affairs, but it did reduce many of those differences.

---

16 U.S. Bureau of the Census, *Historical Statistics of the United States: Colonial Times to 1957* (Washington, D. C.: Government Printing Office, 1960), 9, 537-51, 563-66; Mervin G. Smith, director, and Carlton F. Christian, ed., *Adjustments in Agriculture--A National Basebook* (Ames: Iowa State University Press, 1961); Bureau of the Census, *Pocket Data Book: USA 1979* (Washington, D. C.: Government Printing Office, 1980), 46-53; Bureau of the Census, *USA Statistics in Brief, 1972* (Washington, D.C.: Government Printing Office, 1972); *Washington Post*, August 7, 1986, October 9, 1993, A1, A13.

Senator Nye's analyses were perceptive and accurate in some ways, but fundamentally they were many years behind actual economic, political, and foreign policy developments in the United States. Agriculture had ceased to be the primary base for the American economy; industry and finance had taken over that role long before. He underestimated the importance of foreign markets to the farmer and overestimated the capacity of the domestic market to absorb the tremendous output of American farms. Furthermore, rural purchasers, though still important, could not begin to absorb all the goods and services that cities had to sell in order to achieve and maintain prosperity. Substantial urban and foreign markets (including tremendous military preparedness programs) have seemed essential to absorb the phenomenal production of urban America. Nye's prediction in 1940 that "two- or three-billion-dollar military programs annually" would be insufficient if agriculture became "a secondary consideration" grossly underestimated the 250 billion dollar military budgets of our own time. His explanation for military preparedness programs overemphasized economic influences and neglected national security considerations. Nonetheless, the huge expenditures for national defense have helped sustain an effective demand for American goods and services-- predominantly urban and industrial. The economic benefits derived from exports and defense programs extend into every state. But Nye's North Dakota's share of defense contracts was always at or near the bottom of the list.[17]

Since North Dakota remained largely rural, Nye's agrarianism did not, by itself, doom him to defeat there. With more skilled handling of his political lines in North Dakota it is conceivable that he might have been returned to the Senate in spite of urban dominance elsewhere. But even if he had managed to get reelected, his influence in Washington on foreign policy matters could only have been negligible. The reverses he had already suffered on the national level symbolized the erosion of the agricultural base for isolationism. Insofar as isolationism was rooted in the interests and values of agriculture in the upper Missouri-Mississippi-Ohio river valley, the relative decline of agriculture

---

17 The Nye quotation is from a wide-ranging speech he gave opposing extension of the reciprocal trade agreements program in 1940. U. S. Congress, Senate, 76th Congress, 3rd session, April 4, 1940, *Congressional Record*, 4001-06.

virtually assured its defeat. That is not to say that isolationist views grew only out of economic influences or that the economic bases were only agricultural. But the decline and "urbanization" of the farmer in the United States reduced the political power that isolationists could command. The views that Gerald P. Nye represented were overwhelmed partly by an urban society based on commerce, industry, finance, and labor.

In an age when most Americans were farmers, Thomas Jefferson was twice elected president of the United States. He became the revered symbol of an era and of a way of life and thought. Even William Jennings Bryan a century later could win nomination to the presidency three times on the Democratic party ticket. But the shattering of the old agrarian sectional alliance between the South and West, the growth of cities, and the revival of farm prosperity (and complacency) combined to assure Bryan's defeat. Gerald P. Nye could and did win political victories in the agricultural state of North Dakota. Exceptional circumstances plus his own considerable political abilities enabled him to win some skirmishes on the national scene. He was even mentioned as a dark-horse possibility for the Republican party presidential nomination. But his efforts to restore the farmer to the political dominance he had known in the age of Jefferson were doomed to defeat in the twentieth century by the changed nature of the American economy and by changed world conditions.

Isolationism may not be completely dead in the United States. It is, nonetheless, so much weaker than it was fifty or sixty years ago that it seems almost a negligible element on the American political scene. And insofar as it depends upon agriculture it cannot expect a significant revival. If isolationism ever becomes powerful in American attitudes and policies again (which is unlikely), it will have to find other sources of sustenance to replace and supplement agriculture.

CHAPTER 4

THE AMERICA FIRST COMMITTEE
--A HALF-CENTURY LATER[1]

The America First Committee was part of democracy in action during one of the most terrifying times in human history. It was the leading pressure group appealing for mass support in opposition to involvement in World War II before Pearl Harbor.[2]

When America First saw the light of day in September 1940, Poland, Denmark, Norway, France, and the Low Countries had already fallen before Nazi Germany's blitzkrieg. Fascist Italy had joined the fray. Winston Churchill had replaced Chamberlain at the helm of the British government. The "Battle of Britain" was raging in the skies and seas of that island kingdom. Though the Holocaust lay beyond horizons of the future, Hitler's Nazi persecution of Jews was known to all. Immobilized by the Russo-German Pact, Stalin's Communist Soviet Union (after seizing the Baltic states and crushing Finland) waited in the wings to take advantage of opportunities the conflagration might provide. In Asia militarist Japan had overrun much of China, was soon to join in the Tripartite Pact, and was poised to seize northern Indochina. It was a terrible and terrifying time. No one could sensibly make light of the realities at that moment or of the horrors the future might hold. There were no easy answers to the question of what policies the United States ought to pursue toward those ominous developments.

Few Americans felt any sympathy for Hitler's Nazis, Mussolini's Fascists, Hirohito's militarists, or Stalin's Communists. America's charismatic President Franklin D. Roosevelt had proclaimed American

---

[1] This chapter was published earlier as "What Might Have Been," *Chronicles: A Magazine of American Culture* 15 (December, 1991): 20-22. It is reprinted here by permission.

[2] For a detailed history of the Committee, based on research in the organization's original records, see Wayne S. Cole, *America First: The Battle Against Intervention, 1940-1941* (Madison: University of Wisconsin Press, 1953). For a published collection of documents selected from the America First Papers, Hoover Library on War, Revolution, and Peace, Stanford, California, see Justus D. Doenecke, ed., *In Danger Undaunted: The Anti-Interventionist Movement of 1940-1941 as Revealed in the Papers of the America First Committee* (Stanford: Hoover Institution Press, 1990).

neutrality. He pressed expansion of the sea, air, and land forces of the United States, culminating with enactment of the first peace time selective service law in American history. Never neutral in thought or policies, FDR concluded the deal exchanging overage destroyers for bases in British possessions in the Western Hemisphere. His "aid-short-of-war" policies hoped to sustain resistance to Axis aggression. Millions of Americans, however, worried that those steps "short-of-war" could prove, instead, to be "steps-to-war." Therein lay the core of the divisions among the American people.[3]

During its harried fifteen month existence the America First Committee organized local chapters in most states, enrolled more than 800,000 members, attracted thousands to huge rallies addressed by leading noninterventionists, distributed millions of pamphlets and leaflets, and inundated congressmen and the White House with letters and telegrams opposing involvement in the war.

The committee's leaders rejected rioting and violence. They barred Nazis, Fascists, and anti-Semites from membership, and tried to enforce those bans. The committee used orderly democratic methods in desperate efforts to keep the United States out of the wars raging abroad. The committee's positions on foreign affairs were consistent with traditions extending back to the beginnings of America's independent history and before. When war burst on America with the Japanese attack on Pearl Harbor, the committee ceased its noninterventionist activities, pledged support to the war effort, and dismantled its organization. Most of its members loyally supported the war against the Axis, and many, including some of its prominent leaders, served in America's armed forces. The America First Committee was a patriotic and honorable exercise of democracy in action at a critical time in American history.

Nonetheless, the committee, its leaders, and many of its members took a terrible beating. They failed to keep the United States out of the war. They could not even successfully block specific Roosevelt actions moving the United States closer to war. More troubling, they were

---

[3] Hadley Cantril and Mildred Strunk, eds, *Public Opinion, 1935-1946* (Princeton, NJ: Princeton University Press, 1951), 966-78; Hadley Cantril, "Opinion Trends in World War II: Some Guides to Interpretation," *Public Opinion Quarterly* 12 (1948): 37; *Public Opinion Quarterly* 5 (1941): 323-25, 481, 485, and 6 (1942): 151, 161-62.

tarred by charges that they were pro-Nazi, or serving the Nazi cause. One widely distributed pamphlet called America First "The Nazi Transmission Belt."[4] Senator Joseph McCarthy did not invent "guilt-by-association" methods; President Roosevelt and many of his supporters used those methods with great effectiveness against opponents of his foreign policies. Most leading noninterventionists who held elective office were defeated in later bids for reelection. Prominent leaders of America First carried the burden of their noninterventionist efforts with them to their graves. The committee remains tarnished and suspect in the eyes of most--including historians who ought to know better.

Though he was a member of America First only half of its history, the famed aviator Charles A. Lindbergh was both its most acclaimed and most vilified spokesman. He had his own independent thoughts and chose his words carefully, but he infuriated his critics. He enraged them when he called for "new leadership" in America--though he never intended the use of any but legal democratic methods to accomplish that leadership. And he brought down the full fury of his opponents when, at an America First rally in Des Moines, Iowa on September 11, 1941, he charged that "The three most important groups who have been pressing this country toward war are the British, the Jewish, and the Roosevelt administration." Though denying charges of anti-Semitism, neither Lindbergh nor America First ever recovered from the staggering blows that statement brought upon them.[5] One might have thought that Lindbergh had personally ordered the Holocaust.

It has now been more than a half century since the America First Committee waged its losing battle to stay out of World War II. I began doing research on the committee in 1947--two years after the death of Roosevelt and the end of World War II. In the decades since then I have done research in every document and letter I have been able to locate on the committee, its leaders and members, and its critics. I researched the papers of the organization and of many of its leaders--

---

[4] Friends of Democracy, Inc., *The America First Committee--The Nazi Transmission Belt* (New York, n.d.). Copy in America First Committee Papers, Hoover Library on War, Revolution, and Peace, Stanford, California.

[5] Wayne S. Cole, *Charles A. Lindbergh and the Battle Against American Intervention in World War II* (New York: Harcourt Brace Jovanovich, 1974), passim.

including Lindbergh. I gained research access to Justice Department and FBI records.[6]

From the beginning I took the charges against the committee very seriously. I analyzed them with great care. There were unsavory and disloyal members of the committee. Its membership was extremely diverse, and its loose knit organization made control over local chapters difficult. A few obscure individuals were convicted later for failure to register as foreign agents. Nonetheless, after studying America First and its membership thoroughly over the course of more than three decades, I am increasingly impressed by how clean it was. Close scrutiny leaves an overall impression of loyalty, patriotism, good citizenship, courage, and devotion to the country. Its leaders and members used democratic methods responsibly to influence public opinion and government action on issues of vital importance to all Americans. If one were to balance negatives (that is, the morality of the "dirty tricks" used by opponents of America First versus the magnitude of unsavory or disloyal elements within the committee) the America First Committee comes off vastly better than its critics. The fact that one disagreed profoundly with the views of Lindbergh and believed him totally wrong did not justify accusing him of disloyalty and Nazi sympathies. Those charges simply were not true.

I have reflected on why America First has garnered such an unsavory reputation, and why the images advanced by its critics have prevailed. I have wondered if there were anything the committee and its leaders might have done differently that might have made their efforts more effective or left them less tarnished in the eyes of Clio.

My conclusion is that their cause was hopeless. Nothing the committee or its leaders could have done or refrained from doing could have altered the outcome or aftermath significantly. Conceivably one might set more civilized rules of "fair play" for such important democratic contests. But human nature, raging emotions, and cultural and political differences make self-restraint and fair play increasingly more difficult to sustain.

When differences and debates on important (or even unimportant) matters persist over extended time it is easy to lose control and

---

[6] The culmination of my research and writing on that subject was Wayne S. Cole, *Roosevelt and the Isolationists, 1932-45* (Lincoln: University of Nebraska Press, 1983).

judgment. One may begin by seeing adversaries as simply mistaken, but end by seeing them as stupid, irresponsible, and downright evil. When those differences are further inflamed by politics, and perhaps by sectional, ethnic, or cultural differences, the emotions may become even more heated. That is human nature.

When those debates occur during terrifying wars abroad, the temptation to identify one's adversaries at home with the evil, aggressive, dangerous foreign foe becomes well neigh irresistible. To identify America First with Hitler's Nazi Germany was much too tempting (and persuasive, to those eager to believe the worst) to be resisted. And when the powerful President Roosevelt set the example by associating his opponents with that evil aggressive dictator, the consequences for America First and its leaders were devastating.[7] The fact that FDR was an urbane and respected part of the so-called "Establishment" or leadership elite in using those guilt-by-association methods helped protect him and his followers from the fate that befell Senator McCarthy when he used those same methods crudely a decade later.

And finally, when the values that America Firsters treasured and defended (rural, small-town, traditional, democratic, parochial, and conventional) were falling under the juggernaught of a new America that was radically changing the country's image and values (urban, cosmopolitan, corporate, industrial, creditor, ethnic, outward-looking), the patterns were irreversible.

Many years ago I asked a man who had chaired a large America First chapter if there were any way the committee might have won. He had fought against involvement in World War I two decades earlier as well. He was convinced that once war fervor began to build it was impossible to stop or reverse. Nothing that America First might have done differently could have reversed the outcome.[8] Conversations with others prominent in America First (and in its opposition) provided the same conclusion.

The America First Committee fought the good fight for a cause its members considered vital. That cause and their efforts were consistent

---

[7] Cole, *Roosevelt and the Isolationists*, 257, 315, 322, 411-13, 430-31, 460-64, 484, 548-49, 554.

[8] Interview with Robert J. Bannister, Des Moines, Iowa, September 15, 1947.

with the best traditions of American democracy. Nonetheless, they are unlikely ever to win vindication or even fair treatment at the hands of the greater part of the leadership elite, educators, publicists, or historians. America First failed and suffered the fate of losing causes. The America it served and the world it envisaged are gone and can never be restored.

No one can know for certain what would have happened, either worldwide or within the United States, if the America First guidance had been followed and the United States had not entered World War II. One can only speculate or guess. But neither critics nor proponents of America First can properly pass judgment on the wisdom of its program without speculating about those possible effects--good and bad. Those who applaud America's participation in World War II and profess horror at what might have happened if the America First Committee and its "isolationists" had prevailed assume (i.e. guess) that noninvolvement by the United States would have resulted in a vastly worse world and a more crippled America than we now know. Maybe so. Maybe not.

In the wake of the war in Vietnam, many viewed World War II as America's last "good war" (until the Gulf war). But it was also a terrible, terrible war destroying life, property, and freedom wherever it spread. Nearly 50,000,000 persons died worldwide during World War II. "Only" about 300,000 of those dead were Americans. Even when one tabulates total casualties (dead, wounded, and missing) the American total comes to "only" a little over one million--a tiny fraction of the World War II casualties worldwide. Nonetheless, more Americans died in World War II than in all of its other foreign wars before and since combined (not including the Civil War).

And it could have been much worse. If they had not broken the German Ultra code and developed the Enigma decoding machine, if Magic had not allowed Americans to know the contents of Japanese communications, losses for Britain and the United States would have been far greater than they were. If Hitler had not wasted resources developing the V-1 and V-2 weapons and had, instead, pressed earlier production and use of German jet fighters, the losses for British and American bomber squadrons could have been alarmingly greater than they were. If Germany had successfully produced an atomic weapon, can anyone doubt that Hitler would have used it against London and other allied targets? If any one or combination of those and other variables had been turned around, the balance between gains from American entry into the war versus costs and losses could have been altered radically. We still might be able to look back on victory with pride. But conceivably we might do so from a more deeply wounded America in a less triumphant Western Civilization than we know on this fiftieth anniversary of Pearl Harbor.

A far more terrifying scenario for America might have presented itself, however, if Hitler had not loosed his German military forces east on the morning of June 22, 1941, beginning the terrible Russo-German War. After the eruption of the Russo-German War, General Robert E. Wood, national chairman of America First, put the committee's position clearly and simply: "With the ruthless forces of dictatorship and aggression now clearly aligned on both sides [of the European war] the proper course for the United States becomes even clearer. We must continue to build our own defenses and take no part in this incongruous European conflict."[9]

At a cost of millions of casualties, Soviet armed forces stopped the German advances at the gates of Moscow, held Leningrad against extended siege, checked the Germans in the Battles of Stalingrad, and threw the German armies back with terrible losses. The British and Americans conquered Axis forces in the skies and on the seas, but it was Stalin's Soviet armies that broke the back of Hitler's armies on the European continent--at a terrible cost in lives and material. Nearly twenty-five million people in the Soviet Union (civilians and military) died in their "Great Patriotic War" against Nazi Germany. If there had been no Russo-German War, Hitler's Nazi forces concentrated in the West would have been vastly more formidable than those the British and Americans actually had to contend with.

Before the Russo-German War began, Charles A. Lindbergh predicted that American military involvement in the war against the European dictators could cost the United States a million lives or more.[10] America's actual losses were less than one-third that number. If any substantial proportion of the losses suffered by the Soviet Union had been transferred to Britain and the United States in the West, however, Lindbergh's prediction would not have been excessive. The costs and losses for Britain and the United States would have been

---

[9] Cole, *America First*, 85.
[10] Cole, *Charles A. Lindbergh*, 88.

vastly greater, and the possibility of failure at Normandy could have been very real. The United States and Britain may have triumphed ultimately even without the Russo-German war. But if they had, Lindbergh's prediction would not have been excessive. The United States could have survived such losses--just as the Soviet Union, Germany, Japan, and China did. But the destructive effects on American and British lives, democracy, economy, and civilization would have been far worse than they were.

The next scenario is more difficult to estimate. If the United States had not entered World War II in Europe, could (and would) Britain and its allies have mounted a successful cross-channel invasion of Hitler's Europe in the West (even with the Russo-German War)? Not likely. What would the consequences of the war between the Soviet Union and Germany have been without Anglo-American fighting on land in western Europe? Hitler's armies might have crushed the Soviet Union, but that seems unlikely. Or, Stalin's massive forces might have driven west across all of Europe to the English channel--hardly an appealing possibility. Given the probable Soviet exhaustion by that time, however, that might have been preferable to having Hitler in that position. A third possibility might have (I believe, would have) been a bloody stalemate with both the Soviet Union and Nazi Germany and their people bled white and exhausted. But that scenario need not have endangered American national security or survival.

From the vantage point of a half-century one can even speculate that the main beneficiaries of American involvement in World War II may have been today's prosperous and democratic states of Germany and Japan that were set in new directions as consequences of American involvement and victory. And could it be that noninvolvement by the United States might have left Stalin's Soviet Union more exhausted and less dangerous than it proved to be after the victory that the United States helped to accomplish? And in that situation would the United States in the Western Hemisphere have felt it necessary to spend any more money (and lives and resources) on its military forces than it actually has spent worldwide from 1941 to 1991?

That still leaves the question of whether wars between the United States and the Axis powers in Europe and Asia were inevitable, regardless of what policies and actions the United States might have pursued.[11] And it also leaves the question of whether America's involvement in the war was inevitable, given FDR's leadership, the triumph of industrial-capitalist America, the urbanization of American society, and the erosion of rural and small-town America. Those are separate questions. I would answer the first question negatively, and the second with a probable affirmative. And that gets back to the conclusion reached in the first part of this chapter. The America First cause was hopeless!

---

[11] For an article by an English scholar relating to this matter see John A. Thompson, "The Exaggeration of American Vulnerability: The Anatomy of a Tradition," *Diplomatic History* 16 (Winter 1992): 23-43.

CHAPTER 5

FRANKLIN D. ROOSEVELT: GREAT MAN OR MAN FOR HIS TIMES?[1]

If one is persuaded by a "Great Man Theory of History" or by a "Devil Theory of History," then the years from 1932 to 1945 provide an abundant supply of subjects--of heroes and villains--both on the world scene and within the United States. Simply to list the political leaders of the great powers in those years illustrates my point: Adolf Hitler of Nazi Germany, Benito Mussolini of Fascist Italy, Joseph Stalin of the Communist Soviet Union, Winston S. Churchill of Great Britain, and Franklin D. Roosevelt of the United States. In addition, it would be easy to identify a small army of only slightly less notable individuals from that era--both at home and abroad. Surely the years then and since would have been strikingly different if Hitler had never lived, or Stalin, or Churchill, or Roosevelt.

Among those men, Franklin D. Roosevelt stands as a giant among giants. The most recent poll of historians ranked FDR as America's second greatest president--just behind Lincoln and just ahead of George Washington.[2] And with good cause. Franklin D. Roosevelt served as president of the United States longer than any other person in American history; he was in his fourth term when he died on April 12, 1945. He was president during America's most severe depression, and during America's participation in the most destructive war in human history.

The New Deal included FDR's multifaceted attempts to use expanded powers of the federal government to play larger and more constructive roles on behalf of relief for those suffering in the depression, to facilitate economic recovery from the Great Depression, and to accomplish long range reforms designed to make such suffering and depressions less likely in the future--reforms of enduring value in our own time. Roosevelt used his considerable leadership talents to guide the United States and the American people to a larger, more active multilateral role in world affairs. He made certain that that

---

[1] This chapter was presented originally as a Distinguished Scholar-Teacher Lecture at the University of Maryland - College Park on March 28, 1990.

[2] Robert K. Murray and Tim H. Blessing, "The Presidential Performance Study: A Progress Report," *Journal of American History* 70 (December 1983): 535-55.

internationalist approach won the support of the American people in both parties, that he and his foreign policies did not get too far in front of the people.

Roosevelt's dramatic charisma and leadership talents helped Americans feel hope in the Great Depression, and feel a spirit of pride, patriotism, and honor as they supported the larger role by the United States in world affairs. In leading America to that larger multilateral role President Roosevelt brought the power of the United States decisively to the task of helping to crush the aggressive challenges from Hitler's Nazi Germany, Mussolini's Fascist Italy, and Tojo's militarist Japan. He led the United States successfully and triumphantly in the greatest war against the most formidable adversaries in all of American history. And he did so in ways that artfully and persuasively combined ideology and realism in foreign affairs.

Roosevelt the man, the leader, his policies, and his times provide a fascinating story of great drama and significance. I lived through those times, and have focused a large part of my professional energies studying that era during the past half century.

Nonetheless, for all of that I am not persuaded by the "Great Man" or "Devil Theory" of history--for that time or any other. Individuals do feel rational abilities to choose among alternatives, and in making those choices they do sense capacities for accomplishment or failure, for good and evil. Each individual should feel a responsibility for constructive use of his or her talents. And surely FDR was one who made strikingly impressive use of his capacities for making choices, for making a difference.

At the same time, however, each individual (no matter how great or obscure) is a product of, is shaped by, his or her background, experiences, opportunities, environment, and times. No individual has any control over whether he or she will be born or not, or over the time, place, or circumstances for that birth--whether in primitive pre-historic times or in modern America, whether into Western Civilization or into one of the non-Western cultures. No one has the slightest control over his or her genetic inheritance: the physical, mental, and emotional equipment with which the individual is endowed genetically. One has no control over the choice of one's race, ethnic background, or sex. The child cannot choose his or her parents, family, socio-economic class level, initial religious training, or educational opportunities, facilities, or teachers. Few of us depart very radically from the patterns and directions set for us by our backgrounds, families, and environments. Even as adults one may have little or no control over one's natural energies or body chemistry that may affect personality, emotions, and general effectiveness.

Even a person so totally evil as Hitler may become more comprehensible if one learns enough about what made him--without approving either what he did or what made him that way. Given their total genetic heritage, family and social background, education, experiences, and times, perhaps one should have been surprised if Roosevelt and Churchill had not proven to be great leaders. Given their qualities, experiences, and times, perhaps they could not have performed other than they did.

Roosevelt's mother, Sara Delano Roosevelt, may have recognized this more fully than she realized at the time. She was tremendously proud of her only son and of his accomplishments, but she was not really surprised. She expected much of him. As she wrote on one occasion when he was still a teenager at Groton, "After all he had many advantages that other boys did not have." FDR's wife's uncle, Theodore Roosevelt, put it accurately when, in addressing Groton graduates and alumni, he said, "Much has been given you, therefore we have a right to expect much from you."[3] Those observations by FDR's mother and by his distinguished relative may be seen as little more than trite comments appropriate to their setting--but it seems to me that they point to much larger and more fundamental truths in the understanding of human affairs.

If one is at all persuaded by my analysis, then there may be less cause for cheering the heroes and booing the villains--neither could have done much differently than should have been expected under the total circumstances. The perspective I am taking gives less weight to praise and blame, and focuses more on what the individuals did, why they did it, and why things turned out as they did. From my perspective, Roosevelt could hardly have been much different than he was--given his genetic, physical, mental, emotional, family, cultural, educational, and experience background.

Rather than a "Great Man" or "Devil Theory" approach to the story, it seems to me that America's course from 1932 to 1945 becomes meaningful in terms of evolving circumstances within the United States

---

[3] Frank Freidel, *Franklin D. Roosevelt: The Apprenticeship* (Boston: Little Brown and Co., 1952), 7.

and in other parts of the world in those years, as translated into action by the person who had become Franklin D. Roosevelt. Roosevelt did not create the America of his time or the world environment in which the United States of his day operated. And for the most part he had had little control over what went into making him the person he was when he assumed responsibilities as president of the United States on March 4, 1933.

The fact that Roosevelt was such a flexible, adaptable, undoctrinaire political animal makes my analysis particularly appropriate it seems to me. Neither at home nor abroad did FDR create in his own mind a utopian ideal toward which he was striving, and with which he would not compromise. He was never one to crusade for some idealized utopia out of touch with reality. He was no Don Quixote. Instead, Roosevelt observed what was possible at home and abroad, and he used the political talents and resources available for him to guide the United States and the world to what he thought best within the limits and opportunities set by the circumstances in the United States and in the world of his time. His very political artfulness and realism made FDR a particularly appropriate person on whom to focus for examining the circumstances that made American domestic and foreign policies in his time. Roosevelt struggled to accomplish what was possible (perhaps what may have been inevitable) given the circumstances prevailing at home and abroad in his era. Franklin D. Roosevelt developed certain general values that helped guide his actions, and that he tried to implement at home and abroad. But even those values emerged logically and naturally out of his character, his background, and his experiences.

A relative and friend of Theodore Roosevelt, young FDR was influenced by the example of that dynamic leader--and by Theodore Roosevelt's niece Eleanor whom he married.[4] They and the times in which he was reared helped make FDR a progressive, a reformer, a liberal--but never a radical. Both Theodore Roosevelt and the Reverend

---

[4] Ibid., 85-86; Frank Freidel, *Franklin D. Roosevelt: A Rendezvous with Destiny* (Boston: Little, Brown and Co., 1990), 10-15. See also Joseph P. Lash, *Eleanor and Franklin: The Story of their Relationship, based on Eleanor Roosevelt's Private Papers* (New York: W. W. Norton & Co., 1971).

Endicott Peabody, FDR's teacher,[5] helped form in him a sense of public responsibility, of noblesse oblige.

Though born and reared in a rural-small town setting in up-river Hyde Park, New York, and though his initial political appeals were to farmers and small townspeople in rural Dutchess county, if FDR were to make a successful political career in New York state (and on the national level in the increasingly urbanized United States) he had to adapt to the political, economic, and power realities in twentieth century America. He had no great difficulty doing so. Though many big businessmen and financiers in the 1930s considered FDR a terrifying menace to all they held dear, in reality he may have been the best friend they and their class ever had. His friendships and social ties with them never really were severed. Roosevelt drew those financiers and corporation executives massively into leadership roles in his administration during World War II. And since his death the most cultivated and treasured friends of his legacy, of Franklin D. Roosevelt Library in Hyde Park, and of the Franklin and Eleanor Roosevelt Institute there, are prominent members of those very same social and economic elites.

In the presidential election campaigns of 1932 and 1936 Roosevelt may very well have been a man of the people, but his closest friends, associates, and confidants more often were drawn from the social and economic elites in urban America and abroad. Roosevelt was no populist. Noblesse oblige and paternalism were more his thing--perhaps a democratic paternalism (if there is such a thing), but paternalism nonetheless. Despite transitory episodes to the contrary in the middle of the 1930s, Roosevelt's temperament, style, charisma, tactics, and policies tended to soften or mask class differences rather than exacerbate them. Part and parcel of those patterns was FDR's strong, positive, presidential leadership in both domestic and foreign affairs.

Again reflecting his social background, childhood experiences, and Theodore Roosevelt's example, Franklin D. Roosevelt on New York's Hudson River in the Northeast was never an isolationist; he was always an undoctrinaire internationalist. He visited Europe many times as a child and teenager; he knew Europe much better than he knew America's heartland. His childhood love of sailing, his early exposure

---

[5] Freidel, *Roosevelt: Apprenticeship*, 38-39; Freidel, *Franklin D. Roosevelt*, 8, 10, 16-17.

to the big navy writings of Captain Alfred Thayer Mahan, Theodore Roosevelt's example as assistant secretary of the navy, and FDR's own wartime experiences as Woodrow Wilson's assistant secretary of the navy, all combined to give FDR impressive knowledge and experience on the roles of power in international affairs, and on naval power in particular--knowledge and experience that fundamentally affected his conduct of foreign affairs and war.

Despite sentiments rooted in the experiences of China traders in his ancestry, Roosevelt always was oriented toward the North Atlantic and Europe in his perspectives both before and during his service in the White House. His experiences under President Woodrow Wilson, and his performance as vice presidential candidate on the Democratic ticket in 1920 campaigning for the Versailles Treaty and the League of Nations put him solidly in the internationalist camp--but with the muscle of Theodore Roosevelt's realism stiffening Wilson's more idealistic example.

FDR's crippling poliomyelitis in 1921 added to that handsome, personable man's character, patience, and persistence. It was the fire that forged the steel and strength already building in his makeup.[6]

On the world scene there were all kinds of circumstances and developments that encouraged a larger involvement by the United States. There was the erosion of British and French power that had dominated world politics for so long--an erosion that in effect left a growing power vacuum that invited or almost required America's increased involvement. There were the very real and terrifying challenges to peace, security, and democracy posed by the Axis powers in Europe and Asia--challenges that seemed to compel a larger and more active role by the United States to prevent Axis domination of the world. The Axis states posed not just power-security challenges, but ideological-moral-ethical challenges as well, thereby increasing the ease with which Americans could be moved to play larger roles in opposition.

Those Axis challenges came at a time when science, industry, and military technology had developed to the point where highly destructive

---

[6] The impact of FDR's illness on his developing character is treated ably in Hugh Gregory Gallagher, *FDR's Splendid Deception* (New York: Dodd, Mead & Co., 1985).

warfare could be carried far from a home base--conceivably carried from Europe and Asia to the Western Hemisphere. Those challenges came during and after the great world depression that represented very much a crisis for the capitalism with which the United States identified. And through it all, waiting in the wings, was the challenge represented by Joseph Stalin's Communist Soviet Union hoping to survive and expecting to triumph out of the ruins left by the crises of western capitalism in the wars between the Axis and the West.

In addition to all that, on the world scene there were talented persons in the leadership elites of western Europe and Great Britain who worked assiduously and skillfully to persuade America's leaders of their responsibilities in Europe and the world. Neville Chamberlain and devotees of his appeasement policies had largely written the United States off as a lost cause, and shaped their policies on the assumption that they could not count on the United States.[7] But others disagreed. Winston Churchill and Anthony Eden were point men in the crucial British efforts to persuade President Roosevelt and American leadership elites of the importance of British survival to America's future. FDR needed little persuading.[8] And he had a host of visitors and friends from Britain and Europe who helped keep him informed on developments there, and who communicated his growing concerns and schemes to decision-makers in England.

Given those and other patterns on the world scene, it was hardly surprising that the United States under Roosevelt from 1932 to 1945 gradually moved to play a larger multilateral role to meet and then to help defeat those Axis challenges abroad. Any American leader, whatever his or her qualities, who attempted to lead in radically different directions at that time inevitably would have encountered far more difficulty than Roosevelt ever experienced in his leadership.

In addition to those patterns in world affairs, developments and patterns domestically within the United States also moved President Roosevelt to lead toward a larger, more active, more expansive role in

---

[7] Keith Feiling, *The Life of Neville Chamberlain* (Hamden,Conn.: Archon Books, 1970), 325. See also Wayne S. Cole, *Roosevelt and the Isolationists, 1932-45* (Lincoln: University of Nebraska Press, 1983), 249, 301.

[8] Joseph P. Lash, *Roosevelt and Churchill, 1939-1941: The Partnership That Saved the West* (New York: W. W. Norton & Co., 1976).

world affairs, and toward a larger, more active, and more expanded presidential and federal government role in the lives of individual Americans. Again, Roosevelt was less a cause than an instrument for those developments that had long been underway. Roosevelt emerged at just the right time to become the symbol and instrument for those domestic developments that undergirded America's emergence as a world power.

In sentiment Franklin D. Roosevelt was a Jeffersonian who pragmatically presided over the triumph by a Hamiltonian America. He was a country gentleman who molded and led the predominantly urban political coalition essential for the triumph of internationalism in American foreign affairs. He was an old fashioned progressive-turned-New Deal reformer, who politically harnessed America's industrial, capital-surplus economy to defense and war production to accomplish both prosperity for America and victory over the Axis in World War II. FDR did not create America's heavy industries, its huge financial accumulations, its vast urban and metropolitan centers--but he presided in the White House and guided America's domestic and foreign policies at a time when those socio-economic developments triumphed in America. Given the tremendous productivity of American industry, the huge accumulations of American capital, and the insatiable market requirements of that economy, it was virtually inevitable that that economy would look abroad (and perhaps to defense and war preparations) to satisfy its needs and ambitions. And FDR happened to be president as it did so.

Franklin D. Roosevelt died too soon to try his talents on television, but he projected his charismatic and warm personality with such charm and persuasiveness over the radio in fireside chats and formal broadcasts that he demonstrated what modern technology could do to enhance a talented president's leadership. His mastery of the press conference (in the more disciplined and restricted forms it had during his years) was a model for manipulating and using the press to enhance his national leadership. His charming personal letters and informal White House conversations and meetings were further instruments through which he worked his magic with leadership elites, foreign visitors, Congress, and public opinion. And Roosevelt was not above secret schemes both at home and abroad that left little or no "paper trail" to titillate newsmen then or historians since.

Given those developments abroad on the world scene, given those socio-economic-ideological-political patterns domestically within the

United States, and given the impact of FDR's personal character and style, it would have been incredible if the United States had not moved in the directions it did both at home and abroad in those years. Franklin D. Roosevelt was a magnificent instrument for those developments--a charismatic, political, flexible, adaptable, undoctrinaire, optimistic, outward-looking, "can do" leader. If some political accident had brought to the presidency someone who had not been able or willing to respond to those influences at home and abroad, the times either would have forced that person to action--or would have destroyed him or her politically. Franklin D. Roosevelt was the right person in the right place at the right time--but circumstances in his background, within the United States, and on the world scene made his times; FDR did not. Roosevelt was the perfect instrument for them.

I am fortunate in having available two perceptive critics on whom I can try ideas--my wife, Virginia, and my son, Tom. I asked each to read my manuscript, and I knew I was in trouble when both of them, after reading an early draft, responded politely, "yes, but. . . ." They both insisted that it was possible for individuals, by taking thought, to turn their lives around in ways that broke sharply with their individual backgrounds and experiences. And they cited specific examples.

Virginia, good Norwegian that she is, thought of one of her maternal ancestors and relatives, Lars Skrefsrud. He had been a thief and convicted criminal who broke with his shady past, turned his life around, and became a brilliant linguist and self-sacrificing missionary whose constructive proselyting successes reveal their enduring beneficial effects in remote parts of India and South Asia to this day. Virginia's example was an especially good one to sustain her point--but then I remembered that among her paternal ancestors was Obadiah Holmes who received thirty lashes well laid in Massachusetts Bay Colony before being expelled for his religious heresy. I concluded that she just specialized in collecting brilliant, devoutly religious ancestors who made a habit of doing their own thing.

Then my son, Tom, a teacher, rattled off his list of prominent persons who had broken sharply from what one should have expected, given their earlier backgrounds--Buddha, Saint Paul, Saint Augustine, Dorothy Day, Eldridge Cleaver, Malcom X, Charles Colson, and even Victor Hugo's fictional Jean Val Jean. Tom would have made his list even longer if I had not interrupted.

Of course I had the perfect irrefutable answer to my helpful critics. I explained that we simply did not know enough about the total backgrounds of those individuals. If we had known all we needed to know, their unexpected directions would not have been unexpected at all. I am not entirely certain, however, that my unanswerable response persuaded either Virginia or Tom--or even me--that I had successfully turned back their challenges.

Nonetheless, the historian's craft, the social scientist's research methods, and even the intellectual reach of the biological and medical scientist are much too limited and primitive to measure, weigh, and test precisely the myriad causal influences operating at home and abroad, and in the background and person of Franklin D. Roosevelt. Most historians and social scientists at one time or another have envied the precision and experimental methodologies available to physical scientists and chemists. But historians simply do not command that precision or those opportunities for conducting controlled experiments. I suspect that we never will.

It may be well, however, to keep in mind that even physicists have to contend with the unaccountable uncertainties identified by quantum mechanics. Conceivably there may be areas of human decision and activity that could not be accounted for by even the most miraculously advanced and sophisticated methods for measuring causality, areas that would leave unaccountable room for vital human creativity, genius, and wisdom. I would like to hope that that is true. Nonetheless, I would contend that even if such a possibility exists, the areas in which they operate in the human experience are much smaller and more limited than our popular mythology and personal egos would have us believe.

Given the primitive and crude research methods presently available to the historian, I cannot prove the soundness of my hypothesis. Nonetheless, at the present stage of research methodology and knowledge, I am persuaded that historians and social scientists cannot, with certainty, prove that I am wrong.

If my analysis to this point has any validity, one may feel little occasion to evaluate the wisdom or benefits of Roosevelt, his policies, and their consequences. They simply were. They could hardly have been much different. And even our judgments or evaluations of those patterns and consequences may be shaped by our individual backgrounds and our places within those evolving circumstances. If my analysis is correct then our judgments and evaluations may tell more about us than about his policies. Conceivably there may be some Higher Power independent of human experience who sets absolute values on right and wrong, on wisdom or unwisdom, values that transcend human experiences or circumstances. But I shall not attempt to explore that possibility.

With that caveat and for whatever my thoughts may be worth, from my personal perspective the incredible complexities of the patterns of the Franklin D. Roosevelt era have had mixed consequences--both good and bad, both encouraging and frightening. Even the consequences we applaud may have damaging effects if carried to extremes. And some of the same consequences can be considered either good or bad, wise or unwise, at the same time--depending upon the perspectives and values one brings to the evaluation.

On the positive side there were many laudable consequences of President Franklin D. Roosevelt's conduct of foreign affairs from 1933 to 1945. Most important, those policies provided the massive military, naval, and air power essential to help defeat Hitler's Nazi Germany and its aggressive totalitarian threat to world peace, democracy, and humane values (as well as help defeat Mussolini's Fascist Italy and Japan's militaristic expansionism). And in helping to crush the Axis, those policies built within the United States a spirit of national unity, patriotism, devotion to the national cause, and feelings of national purpose that have substantially faded in our own times.

Those policies also guided the American people and their foreign policy perspectives away from America's traditional continentalism, unilateralism, and nonintervention toward an active sense of responsibility for peoples and states in other parts of the world, and for active efforts to preserve world peace, security, freedom, and prosperity. They extended needed assistance to millions of people hurt or endangered by Axis aggression. They helped provide leadership for the American people and the world as they planned for the postwar era. In that sense the Roosevelt leadership may have helped lay groundwork for what one historian has called "The Long Peace" during the many years since his death in 1945.[9] As a by-product of all that, America's foreign policies in the Roosevelt era helped restore the American (and world) economy to highly prosperous levels that benefited nearly all

---

[9] John Lewis Gaddis, *The Long Peace: Inquiries into the History of the Cold War* (New York: Oxford University Press, 1987).

Americans--and millions elsewhere. All of that was accomplished under President Roosevelt within a democratic framework while guarding and even extending individual freedoms.

Nonetheless, some of the laudable and praiseworthy consequences of the Roosevelt Era may be seen as unfortunate or harmful if one views them from different perspectives or uses different vocabulary or semantics.

Turning to internationalism and assuming worldwide responsibilities for preserving peace and security can also be seen as expansion to build a new American empire. That is, blocking German, Italian, and Japanese drives for empire, and replacing British and French dwindling roles in world affairs, in some ways replaced them with forms of American empire, worldwide in scope--however generous and benevolent that American expansion may have been. International responsibility can also be seen as international meddling and trying to police the world. World leadership and foreign aid programs can be seen as egocentric attempts to remake the world in an American image --undercutting the distinctive cultural, social, economic, and political diversity and pluralism that enriches world civilization. Furthermore, the prosperity that was an incidental but welcome byproduct of military preparedness, foreign aid, and war, may not have been entirely unrelated to considerations of American economic self-interests in which all of us share directly or indirectly.

Strong presidential leadership at home and abroad of the sort that President Roosevelt demonstrated may also be seen as authoritarian, and even dictatorial, in the hands of less popular and less acceptable presidents. Arthur M. Schlesinger, Jr. was very careful to limit his application of the label, "the imperial presidency," to presidents he did not like--mainly Republicans and conservatives.[10] But to put the most favorable possible interpretation on it, at the very least FDR used methods in the presidency that could become precedents, in the hands of less inhibited persons later, that could evolve into "the imperial presidency." Similarly, the reduction of the role of Congress in foreign affairs in the name of internationalism could also weaken a democratic brake on abuses of presidential power in America.

---

[10] Arthur M. Schlesinger, Jr., *The Imperial Presidency* (Boston: Houghton Mifflin Co., 1973).

Methods used to suppress Nazi fifth column activity and subversion in the United States before and during World War II could be and were used to suppress honest dissent from the internationalist consensus. Many respected Establishment liberal internationalists applauded and shared in the guilt-by-association methods that President Roosevelt used to discredit and destroy his isolationist or noninterventionist opponents.[11] But when those same methods were used by right-wing anti-Communist McCarthyites against liberal internationalists, and by the FBI and the Republican Richard Nixon administration for a variety of reasons, those methods seemed a wee bit less appealing.

The national unity, pride, and spirit with which the United States under Roosevelt participated in World War II could (and sometimes has) become intolerance, arrogance, and smugness. Concern can become meddling, compassion can become paternalism.

Furthermore, assuming international responsibilities for world peace and security, can involve the United States in any and every local and regional squabble all over the world (whether the people and states directly involved want us there or not). That internationalism can lead factions everywhere to try to involve the United States for their own local, selfish, power-grabbing interests.

And as no more than a purely personal, irrelevant aside, for a very few (including Cole) the conversion of the United States from a land of farms, open spaces, and small towns, into a land of big cities, super highways, huge industries, multinational corporations, pollution, and centralized government in the hands of privileged elites, is not entirely a shift to the "good life." There is, of course, no way to go back; neither a Thomas Jefferson nor a Franklin D. Roosevelt could have reversed the patterns. No useful practical purpose is served by nostalgia. Personally, however, I still prefer Jefferson's America in which I was reared to Hamilton's America in which I now live and work. Having been born, reared, and lived nearly two-thirds of my life in rural-small town America, I still feel like an unassimilated alien living in a foreign country after more than a quarter of a century here in this East Coast supermetropolis. If circumstances at home and abroad had been different I suspect that even FDR would have had little

---

[11] Cole, *Roosevelt and the Isolationists*, passim, but see especially 456-87, 529-56.

difficulty adapting to and leading the kind of America that I (and Jefferson) might have preferred. But that was not and is not to be.

What I am saying is that even the highly laudable consequences of the Roosevelt Era can be corrupted by lack of restraint, moderation, balance, and tolerance. Nutrients can become poisonous if consumed to excess. The scalpel in the hands of the skilled surgeon may save a life; that same scalpel in the hands of a deranged person can bring death. One pays a price for every gain--and in some circumstances the price may become excessive. Moderation, restraint, balance, self-discipline, humility, tolerance, and wisdom are essential in implementing even the finest policies in the interest of the best of all causes with the best of all motives. Self-righteousness, arrogance, and lack of restraint and moderation can corrupt the best of policies and causes. Much to my personal regret I am not entirely persuaded of the individual's independent capacity to make free choices; circumstances beyond any person's control may shape and determine patterns far more than I should like. And the circumstances I see and the patterns they may be shaping are less appealing to my mind than I should like.

Nonetheless, human kind's innate instinct and capacity for survival, and its often underestimated adaptability, make the pessimists and doomsayers more often wrong over the long run than are the cautious optimists. In any event, insofar as one may have the power to choose between alternatives in our lives and policies, one should try to draw the best from the pattern of events in Roosevelt's Era, but do so with tolerance, moderation, forbearance, and with the ever present awareness that one could be wrong. For the most part, I suspect that that would have been Franklin D. Roosevelt's course had the Almighty allowed him to live on in our times.

CHAPTER 6

AND THEN THERE WERE NONE:
HOW
ARTHUR H.VANDENBERG AND GERALD P.NYE
SEPARATELY DEPARTED
ISOLATIONIST LEADERSHIP ROLES[1]

In the depression decade of the 1930s before World War II, Republican senators Arthur H. Vandenberg of Michigan and Gerald P. Nye of North Dakota were among the more vocal, powerful, and uncompromising of America's "isolationist" leaders. At the close of World War II in the middle of the 1940s, both Vandenberg and Nye were removed from the ranks of isolationist leadership--Vandenberg through conversion to bipartisan internationalism; and Nye through rejection by voters at the polls.

Uncompromising and unyielding in his commitment to traditional patterns in American foreign affairs, Nye was defeated in 1944 and never again won election to any public office or appointment to any position calling for judgment on foreign policy matters. More flexible and adaptable, Vandenberg adjusted to political realities at home and abroad and moved on to provide leadership for bipartisan forces undergirding America's internationalism, collective security, and containment policies in the Nuclear Age. History sees Nye as a symbol and remnant of an obsolete, parochial, misguided, and almost irresponsible approach to foreign affairs that had long since outlived its usefulness. History finds in Vandenberg the wisdom to recognize the errors of his earlier ways and the statesmanship to help guide America, Congress, and his own Republican party toward enlightened policies and institutions for the protection of peace, security, and freedom--the United Nations, the Marshall Plan, containment, and the North Atlantic Treaty Organization. In that sense Vandenberg helped shape responsible contributions to the "Long Peace" that continues to serve Americans and billions of others nearly a half-century later.

---

[1] This chapter was published earlier in Thomas J. McCormick and Walter LaFeber, eds., *Behind the Throne: Servants of Power to Imperial Presidents, 1898-1968* (Madison: University of Wisconsin Press, 1993), 232-53. It is reprinted here by permission.

By examining those two persons in depth one may uncover and reveal some of the elements that led the United States to turn away from the traditional noninterventionist and unilateral policies it had pursued through much of its early independent history and to embrace multilateral leadership roles through the decades since World War II. There were similarities in the backgrounds and performances of the two men, but there were also fundamental differences. Those differences were extraordinarily significant both for the careers of those men and for the future of the United States in world affairs.

Both Vandenberg and Nye were born late in the nineteenth century in the Upper Mississippi Valley Middle West--Vandenberg in Grand Rapids, Michigan in 1884, Nye more than eight years later in Hortonville, Wisconsin in 1892. Both could trace their ancestry back to the colonial period in American history. Both were reared in politically concerned Republican families, and both remained loyal Republicans throughout their lives. Neither graduated from college. Neither was a lawyer. Both had been newspapermen--Vandenberg as editor of the *Grand Rapids Herald* from 1906 until he went to the senate twenty-two years later, Nye as editor of small town newspapers in Wisconsin, Iowa, and North Dakota from the time he graduated from high school in 1911 until he went to the senate nearly fifteen years later. Though both were patriotic, neither ever served in United States armed forces. Both were too young for service in the Spanish-American War; both were married with dependents during World War I; and both were senators and past middle age during World War II.[2]

---

[2] On Nye, see Wayne S. Cole, *Senator Gerald P. Nye and American Foreign Relations* (Minneapolis: University of Minnesota Press, 1962). It is based on research in the Gerald P. Nye Papers and on extended interviews and conversations with Nye from 1956 to 1971. The Nye papers are deposited at Herbert Hoover Presidential Library, West Branch, Iowa.

On Vandenberg, see Arthur H. Vandenberg, Jr., ed., with the collaboration of Joe Alex Morris, *The Private Papers of Senator Vandenberg* (Boston: Houghton Mifflin Co., 1952), and C. David Tompkins, *Senator Arthur H. Vandenberg: The Evolution of a Modern Republican, 1884-1945* (East Lansing: Michigan State University Press, 1970). Both are based on research in the Arthur H. Vandenberg Papers that are deposited in Bentley Historical Library, University of Michigan, Ann Arbor, Michigan.

Both men gained their senate seats initially by appointment--Nye as a young man of 33 in 1925, Vandenberg at the age of 45 in 1928. Both served more than three terms in the senate--Nye for nearly 20 years until 1945, Vandenberg nearly 23 years until his death in 1951. Both were fervent isolationists until after the Japanese attack on Pearl Harbor on December 7, 1941, and neither explicitly repudiated or apologized for his noninterventionist views and activities.

At 5' 10" and less than 160 pounds, the lean young Nye was three inches shorter than Vandenberg and more than forty pounds lighter. His smoothly combed brown hair provided a youthful, almost boyish, appearance. Vandenberg's dark, greying, and thinning hair, along with his formidable build and posture, provided a more distinguished (some thought pompous and posturing) appearance and style.

Both married twice and fathered children: Vandenberg's first wife, a talented pianist, bore them three children before her death; his second marriage was to a Chicago journalist and socialite. Nye first married in 1916 to a Missouri nurse, and, after a quiet divorce in 1940, then married an attractive Iowa school teacher; he had three children by each of his wives.

Both men were serious, earnest, and hard working. Neither was good at small talk and neither really felt comfortable in Washington's party circuit. Neither was ever involved in any financial or political scandal. Neither was a part of or really accepted by the "eastern urban establishment." Both became talented and moving orators--Nye more so than Vandenberg. Both were more effective in committee and in winning press attention than in engineering enactment of specific legislation (though Vandenberg eventually became far more effective than Nye in legislative matters). Both were mentioned as possible presidential nominees--Vandenberg much more often and seriously than Nye. Neither ever won nomination or election to any executive office, and neither ever held any judicial position. Until Vandenberg represented the United States at the San Francisco conference that drafted the United Nations Charter in 1945, neither had had any formal diplomatic experience.

Both men served on the Senate Foreign Relations Committee. Vandenberg chaired that powerful committee during the Republican-led 80th Congress, helping to shape America's containment policies in the early years of the cold war from 1947 to 1949. Nye did not become a member of the Foreign Relations Committee until nearly three-quarters of the way through his senate career when he replaced the legendary

William E. Borah of Idaho who had died early in 1940. But Nye never became the power on the committee that Borah had been--or that Vandenberg was to become. Instead, Nye's greatest prominence on foreign policy matters came as chair of the munitions investigating committee, in his battles on neutrality legislation, and in his speaking engagements across the country (including those he gave under the sponsorship of the America First Committee in 1941).

Senator Nye and Senator Vandenberg co-authored the resolution calling for creation of a select committee to investigate the munitions industry. Both were prominent in that senate investigation from 1934 to 1936--Nye as chair and Vandenberg as one of the committee's more active members. Their views on the findings and recommendations did not differ greatly except that Nye was part of the committee majority favoring government ownership of munitions industries, while Vandenberg was part of the minority that favored reliance on strict government control of private munitions companies.[3] Both played active roles in the background and enactment of the neutrality laws of 1935, 1936, and 1937. Both favored mandatory legislation and opposed the discretionary provisions sought by internationalists and the administration. Both vigorously opposed President Franklin D. Roosevelt's efforts to revise those neutrality laws away. Both failed in those efforts.[4]

Neither Vandenberg nor Nye ever voted for Franklin D. Roosevelt in any of his four campaigns for the presidency.[5] Though both conferred with FDR on specific matters--domestic and foreign--and though both had official social contact with him, neither was close to the president personally or politically. Roosevelt actively courted some prominent prewar isolationists such as Hiram Johnson of California, George Norris of Nebraska, Burton K. Wheeler of Montana, and Robert M. La Follette, Jr. of Wisconsin to win their support for his

---

[3] For a detailed scholarly study of the munitions investigation, see John Edward Wiltz, *In Search of Peace: The Senate Munitions Inquiry, 1934-36* (Baton Rouge: Louisiana State University Press, 1963). See also Cole, *Senator Gerald P. Nye*, 65-96, esp. 71, 92.

[4] The best scholarly history of enactment and revision of the neutrality legislation is Robert A. Divine, *The Illusion of Neutrality* (Chicago: University of Chicago Press, 1962).

[5] Interview with Gerald P. Nye, Chevy Chase, Maryland, July 27, 1959.

domestic New Deal program. Neither Vandenberg nor Nye, however, won much stroking of that sort either early or late in FDR's White House career.[6] In 1940 Senator Nye supported and campaigned for the nomination of Vandenberg for president in Republican primary elections. Both Vandenberg and Nye considered Abraham Lincoln their favorite president and the one who came closest to their political ideals.[7]

The two men had much in common. It should not have been surprising to find Vandenberg and Nye battling shoulder-to-shoulder on behalf of noninvolvement by the United States in European wars, and in opposing President Franklin D. Roosevelt's increasingly bold aid-short-of-war internationalism before Pearl Harbor. Both Vandenberg and Nye voted for the declarations of war against Japan, Germany, and Italy after the attack on Pearl Harbor, and both supported America's war efforts against the Axis during World War II.

Nonetheless, there were certain clear differences and contrasts between Arthur H. Vandenberg and Gerald P. Nye. And those differences ultimately sent them off in different directions on American foreign affairs during and after World War II. Those differences would remove both men from the leadership of American isolationism, but do so in strikingly different ways.

An obvious difference with fundamental roots involved their views on domestic economic, social, and political issues. Both Vandenberg and Nye over time became increasingly concerned about excessive presidential power in general (what a later generation called "the imperial presidency") and about President Roosevelt's power in particular.[8] Nonetheless, before World War II Gerald P. Nye of the

---

[6] For a scholarly study of President Franklin D. Roosevelt's relations with leading isolationists, including both Vandenberg and Nye, see Wayne S. Cole, *Roosevelt and the Isolationists, 1932-45* (Lincoln: University of Nebraska Press, 1983).

[7] *Knoxville News-Sentinel*, May 5, 1935, C-7, Nye Papers.

[8] On Vandenberg, see Arthur H. Vandenberg, "Is the Republic Slipping?" *Review of Reviews 93* (June, 1936):68; Vandenberg to Howard C. Lawrence, January 5, 1938, Vandenberg Papers; and Vandenberg, "United We Stand--," *Saturday Evening Post 210* (April 30, 1938): 25, 79-81. Of central relevance on Nye, see Brent Dow Allinson, "Senator Nye Sums Up," *Christian Century*

northern Great Plains cattle-wheat state of North Dakota was an agrarian radical or progressive on domestic issues. Arthur H. Vandenberg from Michigan, with its mixed agricultural and industrial economy and its combination of rural, small-town, and urban populations, had sympathy for agriculture, could find accord with progressives on some issues, and never had any love for Wall Street.[9] Vandenberg, however, was never the agrarian radical or progressive that Nye was. Vandenberg was an undoctrinaire conservative on domestic issues.[10] During most of his years in public life Nye was to the left of Roosevelt and the New Deal; Vandenberg was to the right of FDR and voted against much of the New Deal.

It has become "conventional wisdom" to equate isolationism with conservatism, and internationalism with liberalism. It is commonly assumed that if an individual were an isolationist, that person probably was a conservative on domestic issues. Similarly it is commonly assumed that if an individual were an internationalist, that person must be comparatively liberal on domestic issues. One can, in fact, identify specific individuals for whom those assumptions were accurate. Nonetheless, as often as not that bit of "conventional wisdom" is mistaken. More often than not in the 1930s leading isolationists were progressives or liberals on domestic issues while many dedicated

---

51 (January 16, 1935): 80-81; *Congressional Record*, 74th Cong., 1st sess., 1935, 79:460.

[9] James Couzens to John Carson, October 30, 1934, James Couzens Papers, Library of Congress, Washington, D. C.; Ray Tucker, "Marked Man," *Collier's* 95 (March 9, 1935): 38; *Literary Digest* 120 (July 13, 1935): 38.

[10] For examples, see Vandenberg to Couzens, August 3, 1934, Couzens Papers; Arthur H. Vandenberg, "An Answer to the President," *Review of Reviews* 92 (August, 1935): 23-24; Arthur H. Vandenberg, "Vampires on the Blood Stream of the Public Credit," *Vital Speeches of the Day* 2 (July 15, 1936): 643; A. H. Vandenberg, "Hash by the Billion! Wanted a Tax-Saving Diet," *Saturday Evening Post* 209 (August 29, 1936): 10-11, 61-64; Arthur H. Vandenberg, "The Republican Indictment," *Fortune* 14 (October, 1936): 110-13, 178, 183-84; Vandenberg to Thomas W. Lamont, December 2, 1937, Vandenberg Papers; *Newsweek* 10 (December 6, 1937): 16; Vandenberg, "Pump-Priming Adventures," *Vital Speeches of the Day* 4 (May 1, 1938): 424-25; and Milton S. Mayer, "Men Who Would Be President: Try to Find Vandenberg," *Nation* 150 (May 11, 1940): 587-88.

internationalists were conservatives. That was the case with Nye and Vandenberg.

Given his mixed constituency in Michigan, and given the unpopularity of business conservatism during the depression decade of the 1930s, it would have been politically unwise for Senator Vandenberg unequivocally to oppose all of FDR's New Deal relief, recovery, and reform measures. And Vandenberg never was one to fall on his sword battling for or against an issue. Instead, the Michigan senator operated from a "yes but" or an "on the other hand" posture in analyzing New Deal proposals.

In 1934 as he faced the voters in his quest for another term in the Senate, Vandenberg wrote that in his campaign he credited the New Deal with advantages that he could "conscientiously applaud," and recognized that America could not "go back to the 'old deal.'" He proposed "to develop . . . the progressive attitude of a new Republicanism which shall operate on a basis of 'social responsibility without socialism'."[11]

When he converted those campaign words into actual votes on specific New Deal measures, however, they were negative more often than affirmative, nay more often than yea. Vandenberg voted against the AAA, NRA, TVA, Reciprocity, work relief, Wagner Act, Holding Company bill, "soak-the-rich" tax bill, court packing, and many other administration measures.[12]

In striking contrast, Gerald P. Nye had sharpened his political teeth in the spirited progressivism of Fighting Bob La Follette's Wisconsin, Woodrow Wilson's New Freedom in the second decade of the twentieth century, the agrarian radicalism of the Non-Partisan League after World War I, as one of the pridefully raucous "Sons of the Wild Jackass" in the 1920s, and as one of those progressive Republicans on whom President Franklin D. Roosevelt depended to help win enactment of much of his New Deal program in the 1930s. Nye temporarily broke with FDR on the NRA, but that was because he saw it as benefiting big business against small business, the farmer, labor, and the "little guy." Like other western agrarian progressives, Nye really was not confident of Roosevelt's commitment to progressivism as they defined it. He

---

[11] Vandenberg to James Couzens, August 3, 1934, Couzens Papers.

[12] "Voting Record of Arthur H. Vandenberg," [1933-1936], n.d., Lowell Mellett Papers, Franklin D. Roosevelt Library, Hyde Park, New York.

thought the Democratic party would return to its old conservative ways after FDR's New Deal had run its course. One of Senator Nye's many criticisms of Roosevelt was that in refocusing his attention to foreign affairs in the latter part of the 1930s the president was turning away from his earlier progressivism and was reestablishing big business, big military, and big government to their powerful, oppressive, and exploitive ways in America. Late in his career Nye became disenchanted with big labor, but his compassion and empathy were always with the "little guy," the weak, the downtrodden. He always feared and distrusted concentrated wealth and power, the high and the mighty, including big business, big finance, big government, big military, and (eventually) big labor.[13]

Appropriately, Vandenberg's political ideal before he entered the senate (the person about whom he had written two or three worshipful books) was Alexander Hamilton of New York, the ideological father of the conservative Federalist party and of business conservatism in America under the Constitution. In 1938 Vandenberg called for a political coalition that "would again put Alexander Hamilton and Thomas Jefferson in partnership for the common good."[14] In contrast, Nye's conception of the good life (like that of Thomas Jefferson long before) was fundamentally rural, agrarian, small business, and small town. Vandenberg's Alexander Hamilton was never Nye's ideal.[15] Vandenberg was no liberal on domestic matters.

In addition to their differences on domestic issues, there were also significant contrasts between Vandenberg and Nye in their respective political styles and tactics. Both Vandenberg and Nye had substantial political talents in their separate ways; they could not have risen to such prominent positions in public life without those talents. But their styles and tactics differed.

Gerald P. Nye tended to put his head down and flail away in direct frontal assaults on his adversaries. His were uncomplicated direct battles on behalf of the hard working debtor farmer, small businessman, and "little guy" against the privileged, creditor, wealthy,

---

[13] Cole, *Senator Gerald P. Nye*, 8, 18, 21-22, 30-41, 46-56.

[14] Vandenberg, "United We Stand--," *Saturday Evening Post* 210 (April 30, 1938): 81.

[15] Cole, *Senator Gerald P. Nye*, 3-13.

powerful, and exploitive elites in the urban northeast. There was nothing terribly complicated, subtle, or devious about Nye's political tactics; he fought for the downtrodden good guys in rural and small town America against the powerful and exploitive bad guys in the urban northeast and abroad.

In contrast Arthur H. Vandenberg preferred coalition politics, with emphasis upon building political coalitions cutting across party, economic, and sectional lines to accomplish shared objectives. In the 1930s he particularly envisaged bipartisan coalitions on the conservative side of domestic concerns; during and after World War II he conceived of bipartisan coalitions on the side of internationalism, collective security, and (during the cold war) on the side of containment. Always his coalition politics cut across party lines, abjured playing politics with national concerns, included an active role for Congress, and envisaged the accomplishment of broad-based unity to serve higher goals at home and abroad.

Nye's political tactics worked best in a homogeneous socioeconomic environment. The upper Mississippi Valley that produced him and the North Dakota that he served had their diversity. There was ethnic diversity--Russian-Americans, Norwegian-Americans, German-Americans, Scotch-Irish, and Anglo-Saxons. There was religious diversity--Roman Catholics, Orthodox Catholics, Lutherans, Methodists, Presbyterians, and others. There were farmers and there were small businessmen. There were property owners and people without productive property. There were differences between the rich and the poor (though those class differences were much less sharp than in most other parts of the country and in most other parts of the world).

Much more striking, however, were the widely shared interests and values of a rural, agricultural, small town, small business, producing, debtor, egalitarian society that felt conflicts of interest in its dealings with railroads, bankers, financiers, cities, big business, big government, big military, the East, and urban elites. Nye operated from an agrarian progressive base in the Great Plains farming state of North Dakota that had little industrial or urban development. On state levels he and his fellow agrarian progressives had no great need to construct complicated political coalitions cutting across broad socioeconomic lines. In battling for the little guy against privilege they found it easy to rally the people on the farms and in the small towns of the West behind them.

Nye's temperament and style fit those patterns. He thrived on aggressive no-holds-barred battles for the little guy against the powerful privileged classes of the great cities in the East (and abroad). Those crusades and political tactics could and did work impressively well on the local, state, and regional levels on the Great Plains. But on the national level in the increasingly urbanized, industrialized, capital-surplus, pluralistic, bureaucratic America of the twentieth century those crusades and tactics were almost certain to fail. And they did--on both domestic and foreign policy issues.

For Arthur H. Vandenberg of Michigan the circumstances, political tactics, and temperament were different. Aggressive crusades cutting across social and class lines would not work in the pluralistic political environment of Michigan as they did in the comparatively homogeneous rural society of North Dakota. And, in any event, that was not Vandenberg's style. Throughout his public career he found fascination in trying to build broadly-based bipartisan coalitions on both domestic and foreign policy issues.[16]

At the very beginning of the Roosevelt administration Vandenberg applauded pleas "for non-partisan action" in the economic crisis.[17] In the 1936 presidential campaign Vandenberg endorsed the "Landon-Knox coalitionists" in opposition to "the Roosevelt party."[18] In 1937 he heartily cooperated with the "bi-partisan" strategy in battling against FDR's "court packing" proposal, putting Democratic Senator Burton K. Wheeler and other Democrats and progressives (including Nye) up front in the contest against the president's proposal, while conservative Republicans (including Vandenberg) stayed back in the shadows.[19] He expected that some of the 1938 congressional and senatorial elections would "be laboratory demonstrations of the means by which a new coalition (built around the Republican nucleus)" could "produce a

---

[16] Tompkins, *Senator Arthur H. Vandenberg*, 144-45.

[17] Vandenberg to Ernest Kanzler, March 7, 1933, Vandenberg Papers.

[18] Vandenberg, "The Republican Indictment," *Fortune* 14 (October, 1936): 113.

[19] Vandenberg diary entries, February 18, March 2, May 13, [1937], Scrapbook #9, Vandenberg to William E. Evans, May 24, 1937, Vandenberg Papers; Vandenberg, "The Biography of an Undelivered Speech," *Saturday Evening Post* 210 (October 9, 1937): 25, 32, 35, 37; and Cole, *Roosevelt and the Isolationists*, 213-16.

triumphant realignment of political parties."[20] In 1938 he boasted that he had "been talking about coalition--the need for a truly national government to meet this crisis--ever since 1934." In his view coalition was "a state of mind long before" it was "a mechanism." He alluded to Abraham Lincoln's tactic in 1864 using "the regular Republican machinery under the temporary pseudonym of a 'Union convention' which nominated a Union ticket, ran a Union campaign, and won a Union victory with a Democratic nominee for Vice-President." Vandenberg was not recommending Lincoln's formula nor a new party, but he thought the important thing at the time was "to encourage the coalition state of mind." With that state of mind, "mechanism" would "take care of itself." It was in that context that he called for "a coalition which would again put Alexander Hamilton and Thomas Jefferson in partnership for the common good, precisely as they once cooperated to save America from Aaron Burr." Though he did not say so explicitly, it was reasonable to conclude that Vandenberg saw Franklin D. Roosevelt in the role of Aaron Burr in that scenario.[21] In 1938-39 Vandenberg urged approval of a "profit-sharing resolution" that conceivably might have served as a basis for accord or coalition between labor and management.[22]

In December 1941, after the Japanese attack on Pearl Harbor, Senator Vandenberg wrote to President Roosevelt urging creation of a Joint Congressional Committee on War Cooperation to be elected by the two houses of Congress.[23] The Michigan senator wholeheartedly cooperated as a member of Secretary of State Cordell Hull's Committee of Eight senators to deliberate on the proper structure for the forthcoming United Nations Organization. That secret and influential committee included four Democrats, three Republicans (including

---

[20] Vandenberg to William E. Evans, May 24, 1937, Vandenberg "Diary," February 6, 18, March 2, May 18, [1937], Vandenberg Papers; Cole, *Roosevelt and the Isolationists*, 213-16.

[21] Vandenberg, "'United We Stand--,'" *Saturday Evening Post* 210 (April 30, 1938): 25, 79, 80-81.

[22] Vandenberg to Mrs. Robert L. Bacon, August 15, 1938, Vandenberg to Donald Despain, February 24, 1939, Vandenberg Papers.

[23] Vandenberg to Roosevelt, December 15, 1941, Official File 419, Roosevelt to Vandenberg, President's Personal File 3529, Franklin D. Roosevelt Papers, Franklin D. Roosevelt Library, Hyde Park, New York.

Vandenberg), and one Progressive.[24] Vandenberg responded cautiously but affirmatively in 1945 when first President Roosevelt and later President Truman named him (along with Democrats) to represent the United States in the deliberations at the San Francisco conference to draft the United Nations Charter.[25] And Republican Arthur H. Vandenberg was the central architect in the Senate building bipartisan bases for containment foreign policies during the Truman administration after World War II.[26]

In addition to the differences between Vandenberg and Nye in their views on domestic issues and in their political tactics (and more fundamental than either of those sets of differences) were differences in the socio-economic constituencies they served in public life.

The America that Senator Gerald P. Nye identified with and spoke for (and that most other western progressive isolationists spoke for) was overwhelmingly rural and small town. It was an America consisting largely of farmers on the soil, and of small businessmen buying from and selling to those farmers in countless small towns scattered across the prairies and Great Plains. The farmers were largely wheat-cattle farmers on the Great Plains and corn-hog farmers on the rolling prairies.[27] It was the America that William Jennings Bryan and his Populists identified with and spoke for.[28] It was the America of Arthur C. Townley's Non-Partisan League.[29] It was the America of

---

[24] Vandenberg, *Private Papers*, 90-125; Cordell Hull, *The Memoirs of Cordell Hull*, 2 vols. (New York: Macmillan Co., 1948) 2: 1656-85.

[25] Vandenberg, *Private Papers*, 139-40, 146-59, 165-69.

[26] Harry S Truman, *Memoirs of Harry S Truman: Years of Trial and Hope* (Garden City, N.Y.: Doubleday & Co., 1956): 172; David R. Kepley, *The Collapse of the Middle Way: Senate Republicans and the Bipartisan Foreign Policy, 1948-1952* (New York: Greenwood Press, 1988): 2-3, 7-8, 56-59.

[27] For analyses of the agrarian bases for Nye's roles in public affairs, including the positions he took on foreign affairs, see Cole, *Senator Gerald P. Nye*, esp. 3-13, 24-41, 227-35. See also chapter 3 of this book.

[28] The most detailed scholarly biography of Bryan is Paolo E. Coletta, *William Jennings Bryan*, 3 vols. (Lincoln: University of Nebraska Press, 1964-69). For a recent perceptive scholarly account, see LeRoy Ashby, *William Jennings Bryan: Champion of Democracy* (Boston: Twayne Publishers, 1987).

[29] On the Nonpartisan League, see Robert L. Morlan, *Political Prairie Fire: The Nonpartisan League, 1915-1922* (Minneapolis: University of

countless agrarian progressives over the years such as Robert M. La Follette (father and sons) of Wisconsin, William E. Borah of Idaho, Hiram Johnson of California, Burton K. Wheeler of Montana, George W. Norris of Nebraska, Arthur C. Capper of Kansas, Henrik Shipstead of Minnesota, and many others before and since.[30] A century and one-half earlier it was the America of Thomas Jefferson of Virginia.[31] With variations rooted in time and region, it was the America of most people who lived and worked and died in what is now the United States during the first three centuries after Europeans began to colonize that huge part of North America.

The United States with which Nye identified was productive, debtor, egalitarian, democratic socially, Republican politically, patriotic, Christian, largely white, hard-working, family-oriented, and had its ethnic roots in northern and western Europe (particularly in Germany, Scandinavia, and the British Isles). It was the America that rapidly conquered the "Last American Frontier" in the latter part of the nineteenth century and in the early years of the twentieth century. It was the America that blanketed Nye's North Dakota.[32]

Minnesota Press, 1955).

[30] For a scholarly study of many of those western agrarian progressives, see Ronald L. Feinman, *Twilight of Progressivism: The Western Republicans and the New Deal* (Baltimore: Johns Hopkins University Press, 1981). See also Russell B. Nye, *Midwestern Progressive Politics: A Historical Study of Its Origins and Development, 1870-1958* (East Lansing: Michigan State University Press, 1959).

[31] The most detailed scholarly biography is Dumas Malone, *Jefferson and His Times*, 5 vols. (Boston: Little, Brown, 1948-1974). See also Charles A. Beard, *Economic Origins of Jeffersonian Democracy* (New York: Macmillan Co., 1915), esp. 415-64; Beard, *The Idea of National Interest: An Analytical Study in American Foreign Policy* (New York: Macmillan Co., 1934): 50-56, 84-88, 166-68, 549-51; Gilbert Chinard, *Thomas Jefferson: The Apostle of Americanism*, 2nd ed. rev.(Ann Arbor: University of Michigan Press, 1957): 132-36, 211-14, 326-30, 351-52, 396-99, 468-88, 491-97; and Merrill D. Peterson, ed., *Thomas Jefferson: A Reference Biography* (New York: Charles Scribner's Sons, 1986): esp. 1-24, 385-98.

[32] For scholarly histories of North Dakota, see Elwyn B. Robinson, *History of North Dakota* (Lincoln: University of Nebraska Press, 1966), and Robert P. Wilkins and Wynona H. Wilkins, *North Dakota: A Bicentennial History* (New York: W. W. Norton & Co., 1977). For descriptions and analyses of North

But it was also the America that rapidly was waning relative to the burgeoning cities of the United States with their booming industries, expanding financial resources, their ethnic and cultural diversity, their sharp class divisions, their more cosmopolitan and larger world perspectives and interests, and their growing power in shaping and controlling American values, political parties, and government policies --domestic and foreign.[33] A person born and reared on the land or in the small towns of North Dakota could feel like a stranger in a foreign country when visiting great urban metropolitan centers in the eastern part of the United States--then and now.

The population of North Dakota never reached 700,000 during Nye's years in the Senate and generally declined later. Fryburg in western North Dakota had a population of only about 300 people when he first located there in 1916--and it has declined substantially since then. Cooperstown further east, where he lived when he went to the Senate in 1925, had a population at that time of less than 1500 people. The largest city in the state, Fargo, had 20,000 people when Nye went to the state in 1916, and had not yet reached 40,000 when his senate career ended in 1945. The state capital, Bismarck, had approximately 6000 people in 1916 and not much more than 20,000 when his senate career ended. Those small cities and villages were largely marketing centers for the rural population. North Dakota was (and remains) one of the most sparsely populated states in the union. What little

---

Dakota's society, economy, and politics, see Melvin E. Kazeck, *North Dakota: A Human and Economic Geography* (Fargo: North Dakota Institute for Regional Studies, 1956), J. M. Gillette, *Social Economics of North Dakota* (Minneapolis: Burgess Publishing Co., 1942); Robert L. Vexler, *Chronology and Documentary Handbook of the State of North Dakota* (Dobbs Ferry, N.Y.: Oceana Publications, 1978); and Federal Writers' Project of the Works Progress Administration for the State of North Dakota, *North Dakota: A Guide to the Northern Prairie State*, 2nd ed. (New York: Oxford University Press, 1950). My thinking on the socioeconomic-political patterns in North Dakota was greatly enriched by Elwyn B. Robinson, "The Themes of North Dakota History" (mimeographed article originally presented as an address at Seventy-Fifth Anniversary Conference, University of North Dakota, November 6, 1958).

[33] For a scholarly study by an able historian focusing on the declining and minority role of farmers in the United States, see Gilbert C. Fite, *American Farmers: The New Minority* (Bloomington: Indiana University Press, 1981).

manufacturing it had largely involved the processing of agricultural products such as flour milling and meat packing.[34]

In Nye's years there North Dakota had almost nothing in the way of defense industries and ranked at or near the bottom among states in the defense contracts it received from the federal government.[35] The per capita income in those years (and most of the time since) was below the national average (and lower on the farms than in the towns and cities). Despite the earnest efforts of the Non-Partisan League and of the state's progressive legislators, the people of North Dakota had little or no control over the prices they received for the products they produced and sold, over the prices or quality of manufactured products they purchased, or of the services they required. Such matters were either controlled on the world markets (as with wheat) or by urban businessmen, bankers, and railroad entrepreneurs residing outside the state and even outside the region--in Minneapolis-St. Paul, Chicago, New York, or London. Quite literally North Dakota (and the greater part of the Great Plains) was a "colonial" area economically--producing raw materials for markets they did not control, and buying and borrowing from urban sources wholly outside their control.[36]

At the same time North Dakota was at the geographic center of the North American continent--approximately 1500 miles from the oceans in almost any direction. Under those circumstances it was little wonder that Nye's constituents had difficulty working up any enthusiasm or felt immediacy for involvement in European affairs. One need not be apathetic or ill-informed in North Dakota to doubt whether the Kaiser's huns or Hitler's panzer divisions were likely to come smashing across the horizons. At the same time they required no paranoia to see themselves as exploited and to find their exploiters in the cities of

---

[34] Kazeck, *North Dakota*, 35-37, 135-95, 230; Gillette, *Social Economics*, 68-74, 86-142, 196-99; Federal Writers' Project, *North Dakota*, 64-95, 121-48; and Vexler, *North Dakota*, 20-30, 141.

[35] *Congressional Record*, 77th Cong., 1st sess. (1941): A1603-1605; *Des Moines Sunday Register*, March 26, 1961; *Des Moines Tribune*, November 10, 1960.

[36] That emphasis on North Dakota and the Great Plains as "colonial" areas exploited by eastern urban business interests is a central theme in Glenn H. Smith, *Langer of North Dakota: A Study of Isolationism, 1940-1959* (New York and London: Garland Publishing, 1979).

America, in railroad board rooms, in Wall Street banking houses, and even in the government in Washington, D. C.

Farmers, townspeople, and politicians from the Great Plains put those pieces together in various ways, and the intensity of feelings varied over time and place, but nearly all could tune in to the general perspectives sketched here. It was a socio-economic-political scenario that did not give developments in Europe across the Atlantic ocean high priority; the very real difficulties that those farmers and townspeople confronted in their daily lives were much closer to home. It was not difficult for them to find the persons and institutions responsible for their difficulties in America's great cities rather than in foreign lands. They had little difficulty explaining massive naval building programs and involvement in foreign wars as foreign policy projections of the "selfish interests" of the great cities of the East.

All that made it easy for Senator Gerald P. Nye to rally political support in North Dakota. But the very farmers and townspeople so numerous in North Dakota (and historically within the United States) were, in the twentieth century, rapidly slipping to a minority status within the United States generally. Farmers were already in a minority in the United States (though not in North Dakota) when Nye first went to the Senate in 1925, and they have steadily declined in numbers, percentages, and power in the decades since. Today fewer than two percent of the American people actually make their livings as farmers-- and many of those get parts of their incomes from non-farm sources. Less than thirty percent of the American people are classified as rural (farming and small town).[37] Despite some advantageous political institutions and talented political spokesmen, rural America for which Nye spoke on domestic and foreign affairs has dwindled to an almost insignificant political minority by the final decade of the twentieth century. And those farmers who remain have been so integrated into urban institutions and values that they are not even a shell of what they were when Nye was a senator from 1925 to 1945 (or what they had been early in American history when Thomas Jefferson was secretary

---

[37] *Washington Post*, November 24, 1982, A3, February 10, 1988, A17, September 4, 1984, A17, May 24, 1987, A3, January 7, 1990, A14, September 30, 1990, H2, February 21, 1991, A1, A12; *Time*, May 15, 1978, 14-15, March 27, 1989, 66-68, October 9, 1989, 30-36, September 24, 1990, 53-56.

of state, vice president, and president). American isolationism has had a multitude of roots, but insofar as it was rooted in Great Plains agriculture and in rural and small town America it was doomed to defeat by the changing American society and economy in the twentieth century.

When turning from the Great Plains and Nye's North Dakota to Senator Arthur Vandenberg's Great Lakes state of Michigan[38] one encountered a strikingly different socio-economic-political environment.[39] Almost everything in Michigan was different--at least in degree. Michigan was different from North Dakota in the 1920s when Vandenberg and Nye first entered the Senate, it became more different during the two decades those men served in public office, and it became even more different during the course of the twentieth century. To a striking degree Nye's North Dakota was a latter day manifestation of the older America--of Thomas Jefferson's land of farmers. And the foreign policy projections of that older America (as personified in Senator Nye) were those of isolationism. In sharp contrast Vandenberg's Michigan was a vivid manifestation of the new America--of Alexander Hamilton's urban business, commercial, industrial, and financial America. And the foreign policy projections of that newer America (as personified in the later Senator Vandenberg) were those of internationalism, collective security, and containment.

North Dakota's homogeneous society; Michigan's diversity and cultural pluralism. North Dakota's egalitarianism; Michigan's sharp class divisions. North Dakota's rural and small town society; Michigan's increasing urbanization. North Dakota's agriculture;

---

[38] Among scholarly histories of Michigan, see M. M. Quaife and Sidney Glazer, *Michigan: From Primitive Wilderness to Industrial Commonwealth* (New York: Prentice-Hall, 1948), and F. Clever Bald, *Michigan in Four Centuries*, rev. ed. (New York: Harper & Brothers, 1961).

[39] For convenient studies describing and analyzing Michigan's social structure, economy, and politics, see Lawrence M. Sommers, with Joe T. Darden, Jay R. Harman, and Laurie K. Sommers, *Michigan: A Geography* (Boulder and London: Westview Press, 1984), Lewis Beerson, ed., *This is Michigan: A Sketch of These Times and Times Gone By* (Lansing: Michigan Historical Commission, 1949), and Stephen B. Sarasohn and Vera H. Sarasohn, *Political Party Patterns in Michigan* (Detroit: Wayne State University Press, 1957).

Michigan's heavy industry. Land-locked North Dakota in the middle of a huge land mass; Middle Western Michigan with its Great Lakes shipping and developing access via the later St. Lawrence Seaway to world wide export markets. North Dakota with almost no defense industries; Michigan labeled the "Arsenal of Democracy" during World War II. Born in the nineteenth century, Arthur H. Vandenberg identified with and served that earlier Middle Western farming-mining-forestry economy and its traditional foreign policy projections through more than half of his senate career. But along with his state and nation, Vandenberg changed course during World War II and the early Cold War. Michigan (and the United States generally) became something new in the twentieth century; Vandenberg (and his foreign policy perspectives) caught up with his state and the nation and became that something new along with them.

There was farming in Michigan--but with a difference. The soil was richer, the rainfall more plentiful, natural hazards less destructive, products more varied and adaptable, urban markets larger and closer at hand, and the percentage of farmers and hence the degree of dependence on agriculture much less than in North Dakota. Important parts of Michigan's industries involved the processing of agricultural products--breakfast cereals, for example, and dairy products. Though such industries were much larger than in North Dakota, they constituted a smaller proportion of the state's manufacturing than they did in North Dakota. And forestry, mining, and shipping supplemented agriculture in the state's economy even in the nineteenth century in ways that were impossible for North Dakota.

Important though agriculture, forestry, and mining were in Michigan, in Vandenberg's lifetime heavy industry became far more important--particularly the automotive industry. With Ford, General Motors, Chrysler, and a host of lesser manufacturers centered in Michigan, the state became the focal point for one of the most gigantic and influential heavy industries ever--both within the United States and world wide. In the depression decade of the 1930s management and labor within that industry clashed violently. Nonetheless, both management and labor (and much of the rest of the state and even the nation) were bound together with the future of that automotive industry broadly defined.

And when defense production, rearmament programs, Lend-Lease aid to the victims of Axis aggression, and World War II itself required unprecedented quantities of guns, planes, tanks, and ships, Michigan's industrial moguls profitably converted from automotive production for civilians to the production of every sort of military equipment to satisfy the insatiable requirements of the United States and its United Nations allies. Referred to as America's "Arsenal of Democracy," Michigan's industries turned out every imaginable sort of war goods in huge quantities. The Ford Motor Company spent $100 million to build the gigantic Willow Run Bomber Plant that produced thousands of huge four-engine B-24 heavy bombers. The state built $778 million worth of new manufacturing facilities to supplement those that converted to war production. In the course of World War II Michigan produced some $27 billion worth of war goods--more than produced in any other state. Though attention focused on Greater Detroit and its huge manufacturing facilities, many other smaller cities in the state similarly contributed to the production of war goods. And that massive war production attracted many thousands of workers ranging from black migrants from the South to local housewives.[40]

The end of the war in 1945 brought reconversion to satisfy pent up civilian consumer demand for autos and countless other consumer products in the postwar era. And then there were the Marshall Plan and the European Recovery Program, the Cold War, the North Atlantic Treaty Organization, the Military Assistance Program, Korea, and Vietnam!

Some of the western agrarian progressive isolationists serving Great Plains states earnestly tried to win defense contracts and war production orders for their constituents. Senators Arthur Capper of Kansas, George W. Norris of Nebraska, and even Gerald P. Nye of North Dakota (among others) sought such plums and boasted of the advantages their states represented for war production.[41] They met with some

---

[40] Quaife and Glazer, *Michigan*, 360-62; Bald, *Michigan*, 432-36; Sommers, *Michigan*, 119; and Alan Clive, *State of War: Michigan in World War II* (Ann Arbor: University of Michigan Press, 1979), esp. 1-213, 234-44.

[41] For examples, see Capper to Henry L. Stimson, August 6, 1940, Capper to Henry A. Wallace, July 9, 1940, Capper to William S. Knudsen, August 7, 1940, Capper to F. W. Brinkerhoff, May 5, 1941, Capper to Samuel Wilson, May 31, 1941, Arthur Capper Papers, Kansas State Historical Society, Topeka, Kansas; George W. Norris to Chester C. Davis, July 19, 1940, November 27, 1940, January 29, 1941, Norris to Clifford Townsend, April 23, 1941, Norris to Morris L. Cooke, June 26, 1941, Norris to General Harry K. Rutherford,

successes, but none of the Great Plains states outside the South had the natural and industrial advantages that Michigan on the Great Lakes commanded.

Vandenberg did not have to get involved in the messy (and politically divisive and damaging) contests between labor and management, or between blacks and whites. He did not even have to come hat-in-hand pleading for defense contracts for his constituents. Defense, war, cold war, and containment required the industrial products that Michigan's heavy industry could and did profitably produce in quantity. Senator Arthur H. Vandenberg doubtless was moved by honest, earnest, patriotic concerns and mature wisdom in departing his earlier isolationist ways and in helping to guide his state, his party, and his nation to internationalism, collective security, and containment. But the wisdom of his ways was more conspicuously apparent in the urbanized industrialized state of Michigan than it was in Nye's land-locked farming state further west on the northern Great Plains.

Included in Michigan's population were many German-Americans, Irish-Americans, Italian-Americans, and Scotch-Irish whose ethnic inclinations tended to reinforce Vandenberg's isolationism. But it also had a large Polish-American population, along with many Finnish-Americans and persons of English, French, and Canadian descent, who added weight on the "interventionist" side even before Pearl Harbor. The unfortunate plight of European Poles at the hands of Communist Russia during and after World War II reinforced the political currents in Michigan on behalf of American multilateral involvement in Europe. In the cold war setting one could even envisage Michigan's German-Americans calling for larger American containment role in the face of Soviet challenges, in contrast to their isolationist inclinations when Germany was the adversary. Author Samuel Lubell had found in German-Americans a major base for American isolationism before Pearl Harbor, but in 1951 when the Soviet Union was the adversary, he asked rhetorically, "If Germany is overrun, will German-Americans vote 'isolationist'?" In the decade of the 1940s the ethnic influences in Michigan generally were on the side of Vandenberg's developing internationalism and containment. And Vandenberg was alert to those

---

July 23, 1941, Norris to Guy V. Doran, November 28, 1941, George W. Norris Papers, Library of Congress, Washington, D. C.; *Congressional Record*, 77th Cong., 1st sess., 1941, 87, pt. 2: 2201.

patterns. Earnest foreign policy concerns of significant ethnic groups supplemented and reinforced the state's urbanization and heavy industry on the side of multilateral involvement in European affairs.[42]

Now it may have been that by nature Arthur H. Vandenberg was simply more intelligent, wiser, better informed, more practical, more cosmopolitan, more responsible, more adaptable, and more realistic than Gerald P. Nye. But one would be hard-pressed to provide objective proof of that--unless one started from the assumption that by definition those qualities identified with internationalism, collective security, and containment per se. Through the press, radio, and later television both Vandenberg and Nye were exposed to information about the antics of Hitler's Nazi Germany, Mussolini's Fascist Italy, Japan's militarists, and Stalin's Communist Soviet Union. In their roles on the Foreign Relations Committee and in contacts in public life both men had better access to relevant information on world affairs than most people. Until near the end of World War II one would not have expected Vandenberg to have been significantly better informed than Nye on such matters. But the states each served (that is, the domestic constraints and pressures operating upon each of them from within the United States) were radically different. And those differing domestic circumstances for the two men projected into radically different roles for the United States in world affairs.

On December 19, 1944, on his fifty-second birthday and a little more than a month after defeat at the polls in his unsuccessful bid for election to another term, Gerald P. Nye took the floor and delivered his farewell address to the Senate. He spoke pridefully and without apology for his efforts to keep the United States out of World War II. He warned that the victories in that war would not be followed by any "golden age for America." He predicted that America would be burdened by ever mounting debts to pay for the military forces essential for the role the United States had elected to accept for itself in world affairs. He forecast that the United States would "be involved in every quarrel between our partners in this new world order," and that when World War III erupted the United States would "be in it from the first

---

[42] Tompkins, *Senator Arthur H. Vandenberg*, 173-74, 185-86, 243-44, 313-14; Samuel Lubell, "Who Votes Isolationist and Why," *Harper's Magazine* 202 (April, 1951): 29-36.

day." Nye contended that the only way the United States could stay out of World War III was "By minding our own business. By keeping out of these entangling alliances. By developing our own markets here in this hemisphere and devoting our strength honestly and solely to the defense of our own territory." He cited historian Charles A. Beard's book, *The Open Door at Home*, to bolster his argument that it was possible for the United States "to find, in our own domestic market and in trade which we can easily develop on friendly terms with our neighbors in this hemisphere, all the prosperity we need for our American people."[43]

But the America of that time (and of today) was not listening. Senator Nye's speech got little attention. It was, in effect, a funeral dirge for his political career and for American isolationism. Nye tried to regain a seat in the Senate in the elections of 1946--but was again defeated. He died in Washington, D. C. in 1971 at the age of seventy-eight. By that time one of Nye's sons had been seriously wounded in combat in Vietnam. His youngest son was serving as an air force pilot in Southeast Asia. And at the moment the former senator died, the United States was pressing on with its unpopular war in Vietnam that ended with defeat after his death.[44]

On January 10, 1945, three weeks after Nye delivered his farewell address, Arthur H. Vandenberg took the Senate floor to deliver the most important address in his public career. He did not mention, repudiate, or apologize for his isolationist or noninterventionist views and efforts before Pearl Harbor. And he did not abandon the critical views he had always held of Franklin D. Roosevelt. Vandenberg did say, however, that the oceans had "ceased to be moats which automatically protect our ramparts." He did urge guarding American self-interests and building American military power. And as he had many times earlier, Vandenberg advanced critical and distrustful views of the Soviet Union's role in world affairs. He called for continued allied unity for defeating the Axis and for planning the peace.[45] (Both

---

[43] *Congressional Record*, 78th Cong., 2d sess., 1944, 90: 9583-89.

[44] *Washington Evening Star*, July 19, 1971; interview with Gerald P. Nye, College Park, Maryland, March 29, 1971; and Marguerite Nye to author, December 10, 1971.

[45] *Congressional Record*, 79th Cong., 1st sess., 1945, 91: 164-67; Vandenberg, *Private Papers*, 126-45.

Nye's speech and Vandenberg's oration preceded Roosevelt's meeting with Churchill and Stalin at Yalta and America's use of atomic bombs on the Japanese cities of Hiroshima and Nagasaki.) Vandenberg's speech won widespread and highly favorable attention. It proved to be, in effect, a triumphal processional for his emergence as the leading Republican spokesman in the Senate for the bipartisan consensus behind America's internationalism, collective security, and containment policies after World War II. Like Roosevelt, Vandenberg was moving with the currents in Michigan, in the United States, and in the Western world; he was on his way to the pinnacle of his career. In contrast, Nye was beaten, rejected, and (with his foreign policy views) cast on the political junk heap.

To understand the directions the United States has pursued in world affairs one must look abroad carefully at world conditions, power distribution, and national interests. One must probe in depth the minds, temperaments, and character of the persons who guided American policies abroad. But one must also look in depth at both the enduring and the changing characteristics of the socio-economic-political conditions domestically within the United States that helped mold American views, policies, and actions on foreign affairs--look at them in Nye's North Dakota, in Vandenberg's Michigan, and in the whole of the United States. It was there that one most clearly discerns the reasons why some Americans and their leaders found the transition from traditional isolationism to internationalism natural and long overdue, and why others (fully as earnest, honest, patriotic, and even intelligent) could find that transition ever so difficult and (in their view) unnecessary and unwise. Since it was Nye and his America that were fading away, he and his traditional foreign policy views (deeply rooted in the soil tilled by Americans over the course of three centuries) inevitably must suffer the disdain and abuse that comes with being on the losing side. And it was Vandenberg's (and Hamilton's and Roosevelt's) America that triumphed in the twentieth century--in both domestic and foreign affairs.

In radically different ways both Arthur H. Vandenberg and Gerald P. Nye departed the leadership roles both had played so prominently before Pearl Harbor on behalf of noninvolvement in European wars. Nye and his rural and small town America were cast aside--along with foreign policy projections of that older America. Vandenberg and his increasingly urbanized and industrialized modern America changed course and triumphed--along with internationalist and containment foreign policy projections of that newer America.

CHAPTER 7

UNITED STATES ISOLATIONISM IN THE 1990S?[1]

It will not happen. The United States will not revert back to its traditional isolationism.

In the autumn of 1940, after the fall of France and the Battle of Britain, isolationism slipped to a minority position in foreign policy preferences in the United States, though the overwhelming majority continued to oppose a declaration of war. The Japanese attack on Pearl Harbor on December 7, 1941 was the death blow for isolationism. It was thoroughly discredited and has never won the dominant position in foreign policy views and actions since that fateful Sunday.[2] From 1940 to the present neither the Democratic party nor the Republican party has ever nominated an isolationist as its candidate for president.

Nonetheless, there has been a chronic uneasiness, both in America and abroad, that the United States might one day tire of the burdens of world leadership and revert to its traditional policies of unilateralism and nonintervention in Europe. President Franklin D. Roosevelt feared a revived isolationism even after Pearl Harbor. He never really believed the United Nations organization could maintain world peace; he had greater confidence in what he called the "Four Policeman" concept that would depend on the victorious Great Powers to enforce peace after World War II. He favored membership in the United Nations partly because that would commit the United States formally to multilateral leadership in world affairs. Even then, Roosevelt did not believe the American people would support a substantial United States military presence in Europe long after the fighting of World War II ended.[3]

---

[1] Reprinted with the permission of the Canadian Institute of International Affairs from *International Journal*, volume 48, number 1, Winter 1992-93.

[2] Hadley Cantril and Mildred Strunk, eds., *Public Opinion, 1935-1946* (Princeton, NJ: Princeton University Press, 1951), 966-78; Hadley Cantril, "Opinion Trends in World War II: Some Guides to Interpretation," *Public Opinion Quarterly* 12 (1948), 37; *Public Opinion Quarterly* 5 (1941), 323-25, 481, 485, and 6 (1942), 151, 161-62.

[3] Frank Freidel, *Franklin D. Roosevelt: A Rendezvous with Destiny*

After the end of World War II, most leaders in Western Europe were more fearful of a resurgence of isolationism than they were of the American imperialism that communists warned against.[4] A major reason Britain's Foreign Minister Ernest Bevin early in 1948 pressed for initiating negotiations for what became the North Atlantic Treaty Organization was his determination to commit the United States formally to the defense of Western Europe in the face of growing concerns about threats from the Soviet Union. Bevin had been organizing the Brussels Pact Western Union accord, but most involved were persuaded that without the United States it would not be sufficient.[5]

The Democratic Harry S Truman administration successfully engineered bipartisan political support for the United Nations charter earlier, for the NATO pact in 1949, and for the military assistance program that followed.[6] Former isolationist Republican Senator Arthur H. Vandenberg of Michigan played invaluable roles in accomplishing that bipartisan support in the Senate and in the nation.[7] Nonetheless, the vital necessity for drawing Republican leadership into prominent

---

(Boston: Little, Brown and Co., 1990), 486-87, 521-23; Robert A. Divine, *Second Chance: The Triumph of Internationalism in America during World War II* (New York: Atheneum, 1967), 114-15, 199-200, 204-8; Wayne S. Cole, *Roosevelt and the Isolationists, 1932-45* (Lincoln: University of Nebraska Press, 1983), 514-28.

[4] For example see Wayne S. Cole, *Norway and the United States, 1905-1955: Two Democracies in Peace and War* (Ames: Iowa State University, 1989), 152.

[5] Ibid., 129-31; Melvyn P. Leffler, *A Preponderance of Power: National Security, the Truman Administration, and the Cold War* (Stanford: Stanford University Press, 1992), 202-19.

[6] The newest and possibly the best scholarly volume on the Truman foreign policies in the Cold War is Leffler, *A Preponderance of Power.* For other outstanding scholarly studies see John Lewis Gaddis, *The United States and the Origins of the Cold War, 1941-1947* (New York and London: Columbia University Press, 1972), 198-352, and *Strategies of Containment: A Critical Appraisal of Postwar American National Security Policy* (New York: Oxford University Press, 1982), 15-88.

[7] Vandenberg's role is treated in his son's edited volume of the senator's papers. Arthur H. Vandenberg, Jr, with Joe Alex Morris, eds, *The Private Papers of Senator Vandenberg* (Boston: Houghton Mifflin, 1952).

roles in accomplishing those and other internationalist postwar policies underscored the continuing recognition that internationalism could not prevail with only Democratic party support.

The concerns were not without justification. Most leading prewar isolationists had been voted out of office during and after World War II. The necessity for unity during World War II, the unsavory image attached to the term "isolationism," and widespread support for bipartisanship during the early cold war, all combined to inhibit open criticism of administration foreign policies. Nonetheless, most leading prewar isolationists still believed they had been right before Pearl Harbor, most were unpersuaded by collective security and internationalist ideas.[8]

Though the term "isolationist" had been so thoroughly discredited that all avoided using the word, there were those who began to speak out in essentially isolationist language. In 1950-1951, former ambassador to Great Britain Joseph Kennedy, former president Herbert Hoover, and Republican Senator Robert A. Taft all delivered major addresses criticizing bipartisan foreign policies. As casualties mounted in the inconclusive Korean War from 1950 to 1953, criticism of the bipartisan internationalist policies and the United Nations efforts there mounted. Though his political effort ultimately failed, General Douglas MacArthur attracted substantial support from former isolationists in his race for the Republican presidential nomination in 1952.[9] The proposed Bricker amendment to the Constitution, first introduced in 1951, would have increased legislative restraints on presidential power in foreign affairs but it failed to win adoption. It did, however, attract substantial support from many who were isolationists in everything but name.[10] Collective security internationalism continued to prevail throughout the

---

[8] Cole, *Roosevelt and the Isolationists*, 508-56. For a balanced scholarly study of isolationists in the United States during the early Cold War see Justus D. Doenecke, *Not to the Swift: The Old Isolationists in the Cold War Era* (Lewisburg, PA: Bucknell University Press, 1979).

[9] David R. Kepley, *The collapse of the Middle Way: Senate Republicans and the Bipartisan Foreign Policy, 1948-1952* (New York: Greenwood, 1988), 101-31; Doenecke, *Not to the Swift*, 189-206, 211-26; Ronald J. Caridi, *The Korean War and American Politics: The Republican Party as a Case Study* (Philadelphia: University of Pennsylvania Press, 1968).

[10] Doenecke, *Not to the Swift*, 235-38.

Democratic Truman administration as well as throughout the Republican administration of Dwight D. Eisenhower.[11] Nonetheless, dissenters who rejected the directions and methods of American foreign policies and who looked longingly back toward policies followed traditionally by the United States during much of its history were sufficiently numerous and vocal to make internationalists uneasy both at home and abroad.[12]

With the death of the Soviet dictator, Joseph Stalin, in 1953, and with subsequent efforts on behalf of "Peaceful Co-existence," there were those who thought security commitments by the United States in Europe were no longer necessary or even desirable.

In the 1960s and early 1970s the long drawn out war in Vietnam grew increasingly unpopular in the United States. Dissenters from that involvement grew more vocal and sometimes violent. Even such a bona fide life-long internationalist as Democratic Senator J. William Fulbright from Arkansas, serving as chairman of the prestigious Senate Foreign Relations Committee, parted company with the administration on the continued involvement by the United States in that war.[13] Though its sponsors had been and continued to be internationalists, the War Powers Act, adopted in 1973 over President Richard M. Nixon's veto, seemed to some to be almost a later version of the earlier Bricker amendment with its isolationist connotations.[14] With the humiliating United States defeat and withdrawal from Vietnam in 1973, the enthusiasm with which the American people embraced worldwide internationalist responsibilities eroded substantially. Many all over the country and in both parties resolved that the United States should never again become involved in such a quagmire. Many feared that with

---

[11] For a convenient summary of the politics of the Truman-Eisenhower years see Gary W. Reichard, *Politics as Usual: The Age of Truman and Eisenhower* (Arlington Heights,IL: Harlan Davidson, 1988).

[12] Doenecke, *Not to the Swift*, passim.

[13] For example see J. William Fulbright, *The Arrogance of Power* (New York: Random House, 1966).

[14] Jacob K. Javits, with Rafael Steinberg, *Javits: The Autobiography of a Public Man* (Boston: Houghton Mifflin, 1981), 402-14; Michael Barnhart, ed., *Congress and United States Foreign Policy: Controlling the Use of Force in the Nuclear Age* (Albany: State University of New York Press, 1987), 39-72.

Vietnam the United States was in the process of turning away from internationalism back to old-fashioned isolationism.[15]

More recently the collapse of communism in the Soviet Union, the disintegration of the Soviet Union, and the end of the cold war, raised serious questions whether there were any further security or ideological needs for United States commitments and involvement in Europe. The challenge for which NATO had been created was gone and the menace of a thermonuclear holocaust seemed a thing of the past.

On top of that came a recession in the United States (and the world), the chronic trade and exchange deficits of the United States, the huge and growing budget deficits, and the almost incomprehensible four trillion dollar national debt. Labor and nationalists objected to what they saw as exporting jobs overseas by building industries abroad and by opening American markets to those foreign-produced products through tariff reductions. The United States, it appeared, lacked the financial resources (and the will) to do in Eastern Europe and the former Soviet Union what it had done in Europe after World War II with its Marshall Plan. It was time, many thought, for the United States to cut its losses abroad and to refocus its already strained resources on solving its pressing domestic problems--the recession, urban squalor, drugs, education, and more. The United States had helped Europe get back on its feet; it was time to turn its attention inward once again. As Europe built its European Union, Japan its preeminence in parts of Asia (and elsewhere), and North America its Free Trade Area,, conceivably each region could go its separate way. Neither the world nor the United States was what it had been in 1941 or 1945 or 1949. World War II and the cold war were over; it was time to get back to "normal."

That perspective found political manifestation in the challenge that Patrick Buchanan and his America First appeal mounted to the Bush campaign in the Republican party primary elections in 1992.[16] And

---

[15] For scholarly analyses on this question see Thomas G. Paterson, "Isolationism Revisited," *Nation*, September 1, 1969, 166-69; Selig Adler, "The Ghost of Isolationism," *Foreign Service Journal* (November 1969), 34-37; and Wayne S. Cole, "A Tale of Two Isolationists--Told Three Wars Later," *Society for Historians of American Foreign Relations Newsletter* 5 (March 1974), 2-16.

[16] *Washington Post*, September 8, 1991, C1, September 19, 1991,A21, October 27, 1991, A20, November 24, 1991, C7, July 17, 1992, A23.

though the incumbent successfully turned back that challenge within his party, most voters in the United States did not seem terribly worried by the fact that the Democratic party nominee, William Clinton, had had little experience abroad and focused his attention largely on domestic problems within the United States.

Perhaps after more than a half-century of internationalism and collective security people in the United States had had enough. Perhaps they will once again turn back to traditional ways that had served the country so well during its first one hundred and sixty years.

Not so! Worrisome as the echoes of isolationism may seem, the bases for that revival of isolationist dominance are not there.

First of all one must make clear just exactly what isolationism was and what it was not.[17] The term itself is an obstacle to clear thinking on this subject. No president or national political party in the entire history of the United States under the Constitution ever advocated isolating the United States from the rest of the world. In the 18th and 19th centuries the term isolationism was never used to describe the foreign policies of any presidential administration.

"Isolationism" was a pejorative term invented and applied in the twentieth century to discredit policies that the United States had followed traditionally during the first one-hundred and forty years of its independent history. The term was never an accurate label for United States policies. It was a caricature of the policies the United States actually had pursued, and that caricature, that distortion, was designed to make those earlier policies appear worse than they actually were so that it might be easier to turn the United States in new directions in world affairs. That distorting pejorative label successfully accomplished its goal.

The traditional policies to which the isolationist label was attached related only to United States relations with Europe--not to relations with Latin America, the Pacific, Asia, or Africa. And even so far as Europe

---

[17] For historical definitions of the term see Albert K.Weinberg, "The Historical Meaning of the Doctrine of Isolationism," *American Political Science Review* 34 (June 1940), 539-47; Manfred Jonas, *Isolationism in America* (Ithaca,NY: Cornell University Press, 1966), 22-31; and Cole, *Roosevelt and the Isolationists*, ix, 6-7. See also Raymond A. Esthus, "Isolationism and World Power," *Diplomatic History* 2 (Spring 1978), 117-29.

was concerned, those traditional policies did not call for literally isolating the United States from that continent. From 1607 to the present people living in what is now the United States have had continuous economic, technological, intellectual, cultural, social, and even religious relations with Great Britain and Europe. The new United States established diplomatic relations with European governments soon after the beginning of the American Revolution, and it has maintained diplomatic relations with European governments from that time until this. The United States authorized its earliest consular agents in European cities during the American Revolution and has expanded and maintained such consular facilities there ever since.[18]

Furthermore, individuals in the United States (including political leaders) were concerned about what happened in Europe--including its wars and power shifts. Emigrants from Britain and Europe fled things they had not liked there and hoped for something better in the New World. But that did not strip them of concerns (positive and negative) about the lands they had left or enemies of lands they had left. Ethnic groups of all sorts continued to have intense feelings about one or another of the European states variously related to their personal or ancestral experiences or memories of the Old World.[19] There were even individuals from the United States who chose to play active roles in British and European developments. The term "isolationism" is a gross distortion of the policies the United States had actually followed toward Great Britain and Europe.

There were, of course, variations over the years, but at base the policies traditionally followed by the United States toward Britain and Europe had two distinctive characteristics: first, nonintervention in European political and military affairs; and second, nonentanglement. Europe had been bad news to most in the United States. European governments were monarchical, they fought wars, and common folk

---

[18] The standard scholarly study of the earliest United States diplomatic relations is Samuel Flagg Bemis, *The Diplomacy of the American Revolution* (Bloomington: Indiana University Press, 1957). On the consular service see Charles Stuart Kennedy, *The American Consul: A History of the United States Consular Service, 1776-1914* (Westport, CT: Greenwood, 1990), 5-27.

[19] For example see Thomas A. Bailey, *The Man in the Street: The Impact of American Public Opinion on Foreign Policy* (New York: Macmillan, 1948), 14-33.

died in those wars. Americans had everything to lose and nothing to gain by becoming involved in European struggles. Furthermore, the United States and its people believed they should decide for themselves independently where, when, how, and whether they should become involved in matters abroad; they should not be bound by prior agreements that committed the United States to war in matters of no concern to them.

One can trace those attitudes in the thinking of people living in what is now the United States back to the 17th century,[20] and it is easy to single out clear statements of those views in the writings of countless Americans in the 17th, 18th, and 19th centuries.[21]

The most famous and often quoted statement of those principles was in President George Washington's Farewell Address of 1796: "The great rule of conduct for us, in regard to foreign nations, is, in extending our commercial relations, to have with them as little political connection as possible. So far as we have already formed engagements, let them be fulfilled with perfect good faith. Here let us stop. Europe has a set of primary interests, which to us have none, or a very remote relation....Our detached and distant situation invites and enables us to pursue a different course. If we remain one people, under an efficient government, the period is not far off, when we may defy material injury from external annoyance;...when we may choose peace or war, as our interest, guided by justice, shall counsel. Why forego the advantages of so peculiar a situation? Why quit our own, to stand upon foreign ground? Why, by interweaving our destiny with that of any part of Europe, entangle our peace and prosperity in the toils of European ambition, rivalship, interest, honor, or caprice. It is our true policy to steer clear of permanent alliances with any portion of the foreign world, so far, I mean, as we are now at liberty to do so;....we may safely trust to temporary alliances, for extraordinary emergencies."[22] And it was America's third president, Thomas Jefferson, who, in his

---

[20] Max Savelle, "Colonial Origins of American Diplomatic Principles," *Pacific Historical Review* 3 (1934), 334-50.

[21] For example see J. Fred Rippy and Angie Debo, "The Historical Background of the American Policy of Isolation," *Smith College Studies in History* 9 (1924), 72-163.

[22] John C. Fitzpatrick, ed., *The Writings of George Washington* (39 vols; Washington: U.S.Government Printing Office, 1931-44), 35:231-35.

first inaugural address, called for "entangling alliances with none." Nonetheless, Washington and Jefferson were not inventing those policy views, and the adherence by the United States to those policies was not due to the persuasive powers of those two great presidents. Washington and Jefferson simply were lending the prestige of their stature and high office to views almost universally shared by the people in the United States.[23]

When the United States turned away from Great Britain and Europe toward other parts of the world those self-imposed restraints and inhibitions did not apply. The United States expanded across the North American continent and built an overseas empire in the Caribbean and Pacific without violating those traditional policies, without intervening in Europe or entering alliances with foreign governments. The United States fought an undeclared naval war with France, fought an undeclared naval war in the Mediterranean with the Barbary states of North Africa, waged the War of 1812 with Great Britain, fought the Mexican War, waged the Spanish-American War of 1898, suppressed the Filipino insurrection, and intervened with military force in Cuba, Panama, Haiti, Santo Domingo, Nicaragua, and Mexico, all without sending United States troops to fight in Europe and without entering alliances with foreign governments. No United States military forces fought on the European continent until it declared war on Germany and the Central Powers in 1917. And even then it fought only as an "Associate Power" rather than as an ally, and it rejected membership in the League of Nations at the close of World War I. The United States had ended its alliance of 1778 with France in 1800 at the beginning of the 19th century; it was nearly a century and a half before it formally entered another alliance with European states (NATO in 1949).

Keeping those historical precedents in mind, United States unilateral military interventions since World War II in such places as the Dominican Republic, Grenada, Libya, and Panama were not departures from its traditional "isolationist" policies. And though technically multilateral, the United States involvements in certain foreign crises (Vietnam, for example) were so dominant that they overshadowed the roles of other states and left images (and realities) that differed only

---

[23] Rippy and Debo, "Historical Background of the American Policy of Isolation," 72-163.

marginally from the unilateralism that would have been consistent with traditional "isolationism." The ending of the cold war has sharply reduced East-West tensions, but growing problems and alienation in the Third World may point toward greater difficulties and crises in the North-South relations. And nothing in the traditional foreign policies of the United States, in "Isolationism," precludes an active role by the United States in coping unilaterally with those North-South crises.

To repeat, reversion back to traditional "isolationist" policies would inhibit United States policies in Europe--but not necessarily in the rest of the world. Given the "tokenism" of United States multilateralism in so many of the crises it has confronted outside of Europe, even a reversion to unilateralism would not block it from most of the actions it might have taken during the last forty-five years or from most of the actions it conceivably might take in the future.

Ideology and the workings of the human mind help bar a return to isolationism. Few ideological systems in the history of the United States have been so thoroughly discredited as isolationism. The view was not simply downed by the informed logic of a better ideology; it was quashed by every conceivable "smear" and "dirty trick" designed to make that once honorable approach seem to be ignorant, stupid, irresponsible, unpatriotic, evil, and even fascist or Nazi.

In the 1950s most informed Americans were shocked by the brutal "guilt-by-association" methods that Senator Joseph R. McCarthy used to defame distinguished liberal internationalists. But a decade earlier President Franklin D. Roosevelt and many of his leading internationalist followers used comparable "guilt-by-association" methods ruthlessly to discredit and ideologically destroy isolationism and their leading spokespersons in the United States--except that FDR used the methods more subtly, skillfully, artfully, and successfully. Most of McCarthy's victims recovered and won the sympathies and applause of leadership elites in the United States; Roosevelt's victims (and their ideology) never recovered. The beating that isolationism and its spokespersons took in the 1940s and 1950s make it virtually impossible for that ideology to regain anything approaching a respected or dominant position in foreign policy thought in the United States.[24]

---

[24] Cole, *Roosevelt and the Isolationists*, passim, but especially chapters 30 and 33; Geoffrey S. Smith, *To Save a Nation: American Countersubversives,*

At the same time that the respectability of isolationism and its spokesmen were being destroyed, massive and tremendously effective nationwide and bipartisan efforts educated men, women, and children all across the United States on the wisdom and soundness of internationalism in general and the United Nations in particular. President Roosevelt, Secretary of State Cordell Hull, many of the most talented speakers and writers in the leadership elite in the United States, hundreds of newspapers and magazines, and countless organizations such as the League of Nations Association, the United Nations Association, the League of Women Voters, and many others flooded the United States with information and arguments on behalf of internationalism in general and the United Nations in particular. That overwhelming and continuing educational effort was so successful that opponents could marshal only two negative votes when the United Nations Charter came up for vote in the United States Senate on July 28, 1945.[25]

That educational effort on behalf of internationalism never really has ceased--in the speeches by political leaders of both parties, in meetings of service organizations, in schools, in newspapers and magazines. When the end of the cold war and the breakup of the Soviet Union began to raise thoughts about whether there was any further need for NATO, the Gulf War provided President Bush with an impressive forum for restating those collective security and internationalist ideas in moving terms. And the wisdom of the ideas that Bush advanced for all in the United States to hear seemed to be demonstrated quickly by the military outcome of that very brief war.

More broadly, all those educational efforts on behalf of internationalist ideas and values have been magnified many times over due to technological and living patterns in the United States in recent decades. Most young people benefit from more formal education than their parents, including more years in college and more university degrees. Both economic prosperity and spectacularly improved transportation facilities (notably intercontinental jet airliners) have made it possible for more and more people in the United States to travel to

---

the New Deal, and the Coming of World War II (New York: Basic Books, 1973); and Doenecke, Not to the Swift.

[25] Divine, Second Chance, passim; Cole, Roosevelt and the Isolationists, passim, but especially chapters 31, 32, and 33.

other parts of the world. Earlier such travel was the privilege mainly of the rich and upper classes (and the men in the armed forces sent to serve in other lands). In the last third of the 20th century, however, the farmer, the small businessman, the school teacher, the student, the retired person, and countless others are included in the flood of people from the United States found in one part of the world or the other. The Fulbright program and a multitude of other fellowship and exchange programs have enabled thousands of students, teachers, and scholars to live and study abroad for extended periods of time. Travel abroad can have negative consequences as well as positive; it is not guaranteed to produce dyed-in-the-wool internationalists. On balance, however, international experiences tend to increase interest and concern (and even knowledge and understanding) of what goes on abroad. It is not the sort of thing one expects will produce more of isolationism.

More newspapers, news magazines, and news services maintain more newsmen and newswomen in other parts of the world than ever before. And those publications without resources for such journalists abroad enrich their own offerings by carrying articles and columns syndicated by the larger publications. All that is supplemented by releases and publications produced and sent out by the ton by federal government agencies of all sorts.

Even more drama (and information), however, is provided by network and cable television that brings vivid first-hand on-the-scene pictures into the homes of most people in all parts of the United States --and do it quickly. The farmer on the great plains may once have been so remote that he had difficulty learning what was happening in other parts of the world (or other parts of the United States); that is no longer true.

Increased exposure to, knowledge of, and understanding concerning developments in other parts of the world do not guarantee that people and their leaders in the United States will embrace internationalist ideas and act upon them. Nonetheless, they do make it less likely that isolationist views will regain the preeminent position in American thought and action that they once had.

Despite the end of the cold war and the breakup of the Soviet Union, the military component still needs to be brought into the mix that makes a resurgence of traditional isolationism unlikely. During the first half of the 20th century no country in Europe (or in the entire world) had the military capacity to land a hostile army on United States territory and sustain such an army with serious expectation of victory. The only exception to that generalization in the early years of the 20th century may have been Great Britain with its huge navy--but no one seriously thought Britain would even consider such an undertaking. Neither Kaiser William II's Germany nor Adolf Hitler's Nazi Germany ever commanded sufficient naval and maritime power even to initiate such an undertaking. Despite the effectiveness of Hitler's Luftwaffe in the air over Poland, Denmark, Norway, the Netherlands, Belgium, and France, it was not sufficient to win control of the air over England in the Battle of Britain. And Nazi Germany never had the long range bombers and escort fighters or the long range missiles capable of striking any part of the United States during World War II. The awesome power of the Soviet Union checked the advance of German forces in Europe, threw them back, and crushed them. But the Soviet Union under Joseph Stalin (he died in 1953) never had the naval and air power (even after the perfection of the atomic bomb) to invade, defeat, and destroy the United States. One should not, of course, neglect the importance of European balance of power considerations for the wellbeing of the United States; and in much of the 20th century the United States did not neglect those considerations. But not until the 1960s and since has any country (i.e. the Soviet Union) had the military technological capability to even consider seriously the possibility of destroying the United States on its own soil.[26]

Despite the collapse of the Soviet Union now, however, people in the United States know that nuclear weapons and intercontinental delivery systems now exist in what was the Soviet Union. They know that nuclear weapons exist in other countries. And they know that knowledge of the essential military technology is not limited to the former Soviet Union and to countries presently allied with the United States. It has been years since the United States could properly feel so secure from direct military assault from abroad as it can at this

---

[26] For an article by an English scholar treating this matter see John A. Thompson, "The Exaggeration of American Vulnerability: The Anatomy of a Tradition," *Diplomatic History* 16 (Winter 1992), 23-43. For one of many scholarly volumes throwing light on American military security and vulnerability during the Cold War see Rolf Tamnes, *The United States and the Cold War in the High North* (Aldershot, England: Dartmouth Publishing, 1991).

moment. Nonetheless, the shocking capabilities of military science and technology, the spectacular speed of its development, and the growing awareness that countries once thought to be too primitive for such military developments are demonstrating surprising potential in those areas, make it unlikely that the United States civilian and military leadership elites will be persuaded that the country can now relax its multilateral security concerns in ways compatible with traditional isolationism.

And finally the society and economy have changed and developed so radically in the 20th century that any serious thought of turning back to traditional isolationism is out of the question.

Scholars have identified various domestic influences that undergirded the earlier isolationism of the United States. Geographic remoteness of the middle west and great plains were relevant earlier; with jet airplanes and missiles that remoteness seems less relevant in the 1990s. Partisanship (particularly on the part of the Republican party) once provided a political base for isolationism. But as the 20th century proceeds through its final decade it is difficult to distinguish between the two major parties so far as their commitment to internationalism is concerned. Both are committed to internationalism, neither to isolationism. Patrick Buchanan's showing in 1992 G.O.P primaries revealed more about disenchantment with Bush policies on economic matters than about any wish to return to traditional isolationism. Even if one were to explain his voting strength exclusively in terms of foreign affairs, he did not come close to winning the presidential nomination--and was no where near strong enough to win election to the presidency. For the most part "America First" was a non-issue in the 1992 primary and general elections.

Other scholars noted ethnic bases for isolationism in the United States before entry into World War II. The anti-British biases of Irish-Americans, along with the reluctance of German-Americans and Italian-Americans to war against their ancestral lands were part of the explanation for isolationist strength. But the intensity of Irish-American hostility to Great Britain appears to have waned. And the inclinations of German-Americans and Italian-Americans (and other ethnic groups in the United States) may depend upon what country in a particular situation may be lined up as friend or foe. German-Americans were not a force for isolationism in the United States so long as the Soviet Union was the adversary in the cold War.[27] A very large part of the immigration to the United States in recent years has come from Third World countries, especially from Latin America and Asia, rather than from Europe. It seems unlikely that those Third World settlers in the United States will prove to be a significant force for any revived isolationism.

Far more fundamental and important domestic bases for traditional isolationism in the United States were social and economic conditions. The United States that shaped and implemented its traditional policies of unilateralism and nonintervention in Europe through the 18th, 19th, and early 20th centuries was overwhelmingly rural and agricultural. The man with a hoe was a not unreasonable symbol of that older United States. Most industries processed agricultural or mineral products and sold in the domestic market. Most businesses scattered across the country on the main streets of small towns sold to farmers and local townspeople. The most prominent and outspoken senators and congressmen who opposed involvement by the United States in World War II were western agrarian progressives from the farming states of the great plains and upper middle west. And small town America continued to think more favorably about noninvolvement in Europe than people from other segments of the society and economy even after World War II.[28]

In the second half of the 20th century, however, that rural-agricultural socio-economic dominance has been replaced by an urban business dominance. The urban forest of skyscrapers has replaced the rural farmstead as the symbol of the United States in the 1990s. Even before World War II rural and small-town population had dwindled to

---

[27] A thoughtful essay on ethnic bases for isolationism before Pearl Harbor is Samuel Lubell, "Who Votes Isolationist and Why," *Harper's Magazine* 202 (April 1951), 29-36. Most scholars thought Lubell exaggerated the strength of the German-American ethnic base for isolationism.

[28] Wayne S. Cole, *Senator Gerald P. Nye and American Foreign Relations* (Minneapolis: University of Minnesota Press, 1962), passim, but see especially chapters 1 and 13; Cole, *Roosevelt and the Isolationists*, passim, but especially 8, 34-38, 50, 128-29; Joan Lee Bryniarski, "Senate Opposition to the Internationalist Foreign Policy of Presidents Franklin D. Roosevelt and Harry S. Truman, 1943-1949," (Doctoral Dissertation, University of Maryland, 1972).

less than half of the total. Today less than 2 percent of the people in the United States make their livings directly as farmers, and many of those get parts of their income from non-farm sources. The lives of that shrinking number on farms often differ little from those of people in nearby cities and towns (except that the farmer's average income is lower than that of people living in urban areas). They read the same newspapers, watch the same television programs, attend the same schools and colleges, and travel on the same tours to visit Europe and other parts of the world. They are at least as alert to the importance of foreign markets for their products as are the workers and businessmen in the cities. Both their numbers and their international awareness have changed so radically in the last half of the 20th century that they no longer provide a viable base for isolationism in the United States.[29]

Conceivably organized industrial labor that is struggling in the present recession and blaming their difficulties on low tariff policies that invite import of products manufactured by low paid workers in other countries may provide a sufficient base for a resurgent isolationism. That is a serious consideration in certain cities and states; it should not be treated lightly either in economic or political terms (or in terms of domestic influences on foreign affairs). Small businessmen affected by the purchasing power of industrial workers add to that grouping.

Nonetheless, organized industrial labor's numbers have been declining and its political clout appears comparatively less than it was at times earlier in the century. The numbers and powers of industrial workers have not eroded nearly so much as comparable numbers for farmers. But neither farmers nor industrial workers (nor the two combined) have sufficient numbers or political muscle at this time to construct a viable political base for a return to isolationism in the foreign policies of the United States even if they wanted to. And for every industrial worker thrown out of work by cheap labor abroad, one finds other industrial workers whose jobs are dependent on foreign

---

[29] *Washington Post*, November 24, 1982, A3, September 4, 1984, A17, January 20, 1985, C1-C4, May 24, 1987, A3, September 30, 1990, H2, June 10, 1992, A3, October 9, 1993, A1, A13. For a fuller account on this subject by a leading agricultural historian see Gilbert C. Fite, *American Farmers: The New Minority* (Bloomington: Indiana University Press, 1981).

markets or on government purchases (including government purchases of military equipment and supplies).[30]

In more sweeping terms, however, the huge urban-based United States economy (industrial, service, technological, and financial) has far outgrown the boundaries of the United States. The products, services, technology, and capital of the economy of the United States go to every continent, almost every country, and to countless millions of homes all over the world. They will continue to do so in the foreseeable future. Conceivably the United States could sustain that massive world economy and still turn back to traditional isolationism. But that is extremely unlikely. There have been those from time to time who have thought that the United States could restructure its economy (perhaps along the lines of democratic socialism) and thereby reduce its dependence on foreign markets and foreign resources. But that has never seemed a politically viable alternative in the United States. Even the democratic socialism implemented by Scandinavian countries has not pointed in what might be considered isolationist directions. And at this stage one need not even mention the "socialist" systems represented by the former Soviet Union and its former allies in Eastern Europe. Present complications and difficulties notwithstanding, the United States economy (and its accompanying urban society) very nearly mandate an active positive role by the United States in world affairs. It can do no other.

Perhaps one should never say never. Change is constant. What is will pass. And historians may not necessarily be the most perceptive in anticipating forthcoming changes. Nonetheless, contrary to common mythology, history does not repeat itself--at least not in identical forms. Short of fundamental or cataclysmic changes within the United States (far more severe than the present recession) or on the world scene (even more striking than the end of the cold war), in the foreseeable future the United States will not turn back to the policies of noninvolvement in European affairs and unilateralism (policies commonly called isolationism in the 20th century).

---

[30] Robert H. Zieger, *American Workers, American Unions, 1920-1985* (Baltimore, MD: Johns Hopkins University Press, 1986), 193-99; Thomas B. Edsall, *The New Politics of Inequality* (New York: Norton, 1984).

INDEX